YORK NOTES

General Editors: Professor A.N. Jeffares (*University of Stirling*) & Professor Suheil Bushrui (*American University of Beirut*)

William Shakespeare
RICHARD III

Notes by Charles Barber

MA (CAMBRIDGE) PH D (GOTHENBURG)
Formerly Reader in English Language and Literature, University of Leeds

LONGMAN
YORK PRESS

YORK PRESS
Immeuble Esseily, Place Riad Solh, Beirut

ADDISON WESLEY LONGMAN LIMITED
Edinburgh Gate, Harlow,
Essex CM20 2JE, England
Associated companies, branches and representatives
throughout the world

First published 1981
Thirteenth impression 1998

ISBN 0-582-02301-7

Printed in Singapore (PH)

Contents

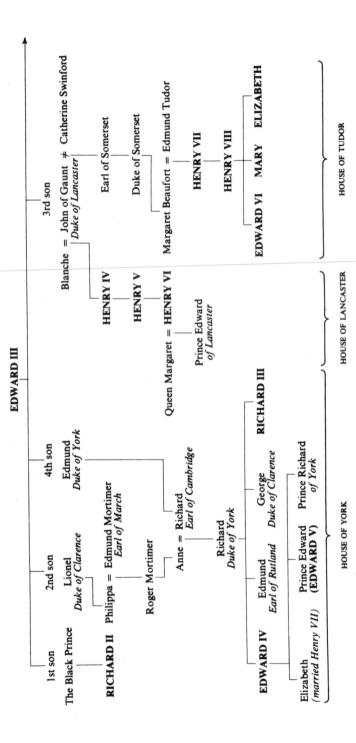

A SKELETON FAMILY TREE, SHOWING THE HOUSES OF YORK, LANCASTER AND TUDOR

For greater clarity, the fourth son of Edward III is shown before his third son

EDWARD III

1st son — The Black Prince — RICHARD II

2nd son — Lionel *Duke of Clarence* — Philippa = Edmund Mortimer *Earl of March* — Roger Mortimer — Anne = Richard *Earl of Cambridge*

4th son — Edmund *Duke of York* — Richard *Duke of York*

Richard *Duke of York* → George *Duke of Clarence*, Prince Richard *of York*, RICHARD III, Edmund *Earl of Rutland*, Prince Edward (**EDWARD V**), **EDWARD IV**, Elizabeth *(married Henry VII)*

HOUSE OF YORK

3rd son — Blanche = John of Gaunt ≠ Catherine Swinford *Duke of Lancaster*

HENRY IV — **HENRY V** — Queen Margaret = **HENRY VI** — Prince Edward *of Lancaster*

HOUSE OF LANCASTER

Earl of Somerset — Duke of Somerset — Margaret Beaufort = Edmund Tudor — **HENRY VII** — **HENRY VIII** — **EDWARD VI**, **MARY**, **ELIZABETH**

HOUSE OF TUDOR

Part 1

Introduction

The historical background

William Shakespeare lived from 1564 to 1616, during which time there was a period of relative stability and peace in English society. This period of calm occurred between two periods of tumult and change, the Reformation and the Civil Wars. The Reformation was the breaking away of the English Church from the authority of the Pope in Rome, followed by changes in doctrine and church services. It was started by King Henry VIII about twenty-five years before Shakespeare was born, and involved a period of conflict between Protestants (reformers) and Catholics (traditionalists) which broke out at times into armed rebellion, both under the Protestant King Edward VI (1547–53) and under the Catholic Queen Mary (1553–8). Twenty-five years after Shakespeare's death, England was just entering the Civil Wars (1640–9), the armed struggle between King and Parliament which can well be called the English Revolution.

The Reformation and the Civil Wars were major stages in the change from feudal England to capitalist England. In Shakespeare's lifetime, English society still had feudal forms and a feudal social structure, but within this society there were powerful forces for change. There were Puritans, who wished to carry the Reformation further and to abolish bishops; there were scientists, who were undermining traditional views of the universe; and above all there were capitalist landlords and merchants who, especially in south-eastern England, were trying to break down or evade the customary controls on economic activity.

The age of Shakespeare, then, was one both of stability and of tension; and both the stability and the tension exercised a strong effect on his art. The period of relative calm and prosperity in the second half of the reign of Queen Elizabeth I (1558–1603) provided material conditions in which a professional English theatre could flourish; the social tensions provided, if only indirectly, the subject matter for the greatest plays of this theatre.

The social hierarchy

In English society in Shakespeare's time there was a well-defined hierarchy, that is, a series of graded ranks. In theory, every individual belonged to one of these grades. Four main grades were usually recognised: (1) gentlemen, (2) citizens, (3) yeomen, and (4) artificers and labourers. The second group, citizens, did not include everybody who worked in a town, but only those who were masters of their trade; it thus excluded journeymen (craftsmen hired by the masters, and paid a daily wage) and apprentices. The third group, yeomen, were substantial farmers, who held land worth at least forty shillings a year; unlike gentlemen-landlords, they might engage in manual labour on their farms. The fourth group included all kinds of wage-labourers, and peasants who were not substantial enough to qualify as yeomen.

The first group, that of the gentlemen, was subdivided into a considerable number of grades. At the top was the prince (or sovereign); then came the peers or nobility (dukes, marquesses, earls, viscounts, barons); and finally the lesser gentry (knights, esquires, gentlemen). It will be noticed that the word 'gentleman', which was of enormous importance in Shakespeare's England, had more than one meaning. First, it can mean anybody in the top group of society, including knights, noblemen, and even the monarch: in *Richard III*, Sir James Tyrrel (a knight) is referred to as a gentleman (IV.2.36), and so is Prince Edward, the son of King Henry VI (I.2.242). But secondly, *gentleman* was used as the name of one sub-group of this class, namely the lowest, the simple gentleman; Richard III uses the word in this sense when he plans to marry off Clarence's daughter to 'some mean poor gentleman' (IV.2.52).

The gentlemen (in the wide sense) probably represented only about five per cent of the population, but they had almost all the power, and many privileges. Essentially they were a land-owning class, but certain other groups were also recognised as gentlemen, for example army officers of the rank of captain and above, and people with university degrees (though there was always some dispute about the exact boundaries).

When we read Shakespeare, we have to remember that words such as *gentle* and *noble* often refer to social class, as do words like *mechanic*, *base*, *common*, and *vulgar* (all of which refer to people of the lowest class). In *Richard III*, Richard encourages his army before the Battle of Bosworth with the words:

Fight, gentlemen of England! Fight, bold yeomen!
(V.3.339)

The two halves of the line are addressed to different social groups in his army. Earlier in the play, Queen Margaret says to Richard:

Ah, gentle villain, do not turn away!
(I.3.162)

Here there is a double pun: *gentle* means (a) well-born, having the status of a gentleman, (b) having the character appropriate to a gentleman, generous, mild; while *villain* means (a) peasant, low-born rustic, (b) scoundrel, criminal. Margaret is implying that, although Richard is of noble birth, he lacks the qualities of character that a nobleman should have.

In practice, the social system was more complicated than the four-class scheme suggests. Moreover, the class barriers were not rigid, and there was movement both up and down. Indeed, in the sixteenth century there was a whole new nobility, created by the Tudor monarchs, alongside the ancient nobility, and many successful merchants and lawyers climbed into the ranks of the gentry. A common topic of debate was inherited versus acquired nobility: was it better to have inherited a noble title, or to have won it by your own ability? The ancient gentry often despised the new, and this is reflected in *Richard III*, where Richard sneers at Queen Elizabeth and her relatives as parvenus.

Despite the complications, the status of gentlemen was a key one, and the reader of Shakespeare has to learn to respond to the implications of words such as 'gentle'.

The Elizabethan world-view

The dominant beliefs of the age reflect the hierarchical forms of society: the idea of order or hierarchy is central. The whole universe formed one vast hierarchy, from God down to the minerals; there were no gaps in the chain, and everything had a place in it. Below God were the angels, arranged in nine ranks; then human beings, arranged in social classes; then three grades of animal life; then vegetable life; and finally inanimate objects. Man was a key point in the chain, the link between matter and spirit, and he constituted a kind of miniature universe, a microcosm. There were detailed resemblances between his body and the universe. For example, the universe was believed to be made of four elements (earth, air, fire, water), composed of pairs of four fundamental qualities (hot, cold, moist, dry). Similarly, a man's temperament was thought to be determined by the balance within him of four fluids, called humours (melancholy, blood, choler, phlegm), composed of the same four qualities. The hierarchies that composed the universe were similar to one another in various ways: as God was head of the universe, so the king was head of society, the lion was the king of beasts, the eagle the king of birds, the sun the chief of the heavenly bodies, the head the chief part of the human body, and so on.

According to this world-view, it is natural for people to accept their place in the social hierarchy: it is natural (and therefore right) for subjects to obey their king, women to obey their husbands, children to obey their parents. The king is God's deputy on earth, and rebellion against him is rebellion against God, and therefore a sin. The doctrine of the Divine Right of Kings held that a monarch derived his authority from God, and was responsible only to God, not to his subjects. It was however recognised that there were usurpers and tyrants (like Shakespeare's Richard III) to whom the theory did not apply.

Man's salvation

There were bitter religious disputes in sixteenth-century England, but it was still taken for granted that everybody in the country was a Christian and accepted a certain religious view of the universe. According to this view, the universe had a purpose: it had been created for the benefit of mankind, and it was the stage for the drama of man's salvation. When God created the first human beings, Adam and Eve, they were perfect and sinless. Then came the Fall of Man: at the instigation of the serpent (identified by theologians with Satan), Adam and Eve disobeyed God and became sinful. Without sin, mankind would have been immortal, but the result of sin is death. Moreover, sinfulness is inherited, so that all mankind (who are descended from Adam and Eve) are inherently sinful, and subject to death. After death the soul lives on, and may be rewarded or punished by God. The punishment for sin is eternal damnation in Hell, but God has redeemed mankind from this punishment: he himself came to earth as a man, Jesus Christ, and suffered death by crucifixion, thus taking upon himself the punishment due to mankind. All those who believe in him are forgiven their sins, and will escape Hell, going instead to eternal bliss in Heaven. At the end of the world will come the Last Judgement (or Doomsday): God, surrounded by his angels, will descend to the earth; the dead will arise from their graves, and God will sit in judgement on every member of mankind.

The middle way of Queen Elizabeth I

The social and political conflicts of the age tended to be fought out in the arena of religion. On the one hand there were the Puritans, who wished to push the Reformation further, and to remove from the Church what they considered to be relics of paganism. On the other hand there were the Catholics, who wanted to restore older forms of worship and once again recognise the Pope as the head of the English Church. Catholicism was illegal in England in Elizabeth's reign, since Catholics did not recognise Elizabeth as the legitimate queen; but it was still a strong force, especially in the more feudal north, while puritanism was strongest in the south-east and in the great sea-ports. Between these extremes there was a whole spectrum of intermediate opinion.

Elizabeth maintained her position by constant compromise, and by holding the balance of power between the contending parties. Her policy of compromise is illustrated by her Church settlement. It was still universally accepted that there could be only one Church in England, compulsory for all; the disputes were about its nature. Elizabeth's settlement tried to make the Church of England acceptable to as many people as possible. The monarch was head of the Church, and it was governed by bishops, thus maintaining hierarchy; but many disputed points of doctrine were deliberately left ambiguous. From most of the population, Elizabeth demanded only an outward conformity, saying that she had no 'windows on men's souls'. The Church of England, not unnaturally, was attacked from both sides, Catholic and Puritan, but aimed at conciliating the moderates in both camps.

In the 1580s, after some years of relative stability in England, there was a growing sense of national unity and national pride. These feelings were greatly encouraged by the events of 1588. In that year, Spain, the most powerful of the Catholic countries, attempted to invade England with an army carried in an enormous fleet, the so-called Great Armada. The Armada was crushingly defeated by the English navy: of 129 ships that left Spain, only 54 battered wrecks returned. But, what was perhaps more important, the expected Catholic revolt in England did not take place. Nobody knew how many secret Catholics there were in England, nor what percentage of them belonged to the militant wing that advocated armed rebellion. But the ruling classes certainly feared such a revolt, and it was this fear that led many Puritans and many capitalist landlords to support the crown. When the Spanish fleet sailed up the English Channel, many people expected a major rising; but in the event the Catholic rebellion did not materialise; and the euphoria of the years following 1588, the exhilaration and the sense of national unity, were surely due as much to this fact as to the defeat of the Armada.

The equilibrium of the 1590s

But the moment of national unity contained the seeds of its own decay. If there was no longer any danger of a Catholic counter-revolution, there was no longer any need for Puritans or capitalist gentry to support the Crown: and the stage was set for the coming conflict between king and parliament. But for ten or fifteen years after the Armada there was an uneasy truce, partly because of the long war against Spain, partly because many men were content to wait for the old Queen to die, hoping for new policies from her successor. So there was a period of balance or equilibrium, like the interval between an ebbing and a flowing tide. Then, in the early years of the seventeenth century, social forces became more and more polarised, and the struggle for power began between king and parliament, to culminate in the Civil Wars.

It will be seen that Shakespeare's career as a dramatist, which ran from about 1590 to 1612, came at a critical point in English history. The first decade of his writing occurred in the upsurge of national confidence and exhilaration which followed the defeat of the Armada, when class-conflicts were temporarily damped down and there was a strong sense of national unity. In the theatre, these feelings are reflected in the popularity of history plays, which usually handle the events of England's past in a patriotic manner; they are a common theatrical type until about 1605, after which time they almost entirely disappear. Shakespeare's *Richard III* (*c.*1593) belongs to this period, and can be seen as a celebration of national unity and peace: it looks back to the horrors of civil war, and forward to the unity and prosperity of Shakespeare's own time. In the 1590s, besides history plays, Shakespeare mainly wrote romantic comedies, tragedies being exceptional. But in about 1600, when England began to move into a period of social crisis and conflict, Shakespeare's work underwent a marked change: between 1600 and 1610 his works were predominantly tragedies; even plays which are nominally comedies are in fact really problem plays. In the plays of this period, Shakespeare explored the growing social crisis of the time, not directly, but through ideas, attitudes, and conflicting world-views.

The Elizabethan drama

Shakespeare was not an isolated phenomenon: he was the greatest figure in a theatrical industry which employed dozens of writers and produced hundreds of plays. Even if Shakespeare had never lived, the period from 1585 to 1625 would still have been a great age of English drama. The basis for this achievement was the existence of a number of permanent theatres and theatrical companies in London, and of a large audience for them. The theatres performed every afternoon except Sunday, and put on a different play every day: a new play was not given a continuous run, but was revived for single performances, the intervals between revivals getting greater as its popularity declined. The standards of performance were high: the London theatre was a full-time professional theatre, and its actors were famous all over northern Europe.

The first two specially built public theatres in London, the Theatre and the Curtain, were built in 1576. At that time Shakespeare was twelve years old, and by the time he reached manhood the London theatre was an established institution, with its companies, its audiences, its conventions—an institution sufficiently stable and respectable to attract to its services an ambitious young man from the provinces with literary inclinations.

The theatres built in 1576 did not spring up suddenly out of nothing: there was already a centuries-old tradition of popular drama in England—religious plays, folk-festival plays, moral plays with allegorical characters. Alongside these arose in the sixteenth century a more learned drama: at schools and universities, students performed plays by Latin authors (Terence, Plautus, Seneca), and then English plays in imitation of them. There were also various kinds of elaborate entertainment at court, and by the 1580s elegant and stylish prose comedies were being performed by boy-companies at the court of Elizabeth I. So in the second half of the sixteenth century there was a profusion of dramatic traditions in England—religious and secular, popular and polite, academic and courtly.

One consequence of the period of national unity and social equilibrium in the 1580s and 1590s was that the theatre became genuinely national, addressing itself to all classes of society. University men went into the popular theatre as writers, and brought about a fusion of the popular and academic and courtly traditions. An example of this is Christopher Marlowe (1564–93), who went to the University of Cambridge, taking his BA degree in 1584 and his MA in 1587; he then wrote a series of famous and successful dramas for the London theatre, of which the best-known is *Dr Faustus* (*c.* 1592). The fusion of traditions was possible because there was also a fusion of audiences: the theatre that Shakespeare wrote for represented all the classes of London, from noblemen down to labourers, and their womenfolk. And when Shakespeare's company performed for the Queen at court, they acted for her the same plays as those performed for the audience of their public theatre.

With this fusion of traditions, the great period of the English drama begins. The broad audience was a source of strength. For maximum success, plays needed the sophistication and elegance demanded by the gentry in the audience, but also the directness of appeal and the entertainment value demanded by the uneducated. The fact that the best dramatists of the age could fulfil these requirements suggests that the different social groups in the audience had a remarkable community of outlook and interests.

But, like the equilibrium in society, the wide audience of Shakespeare's theatre was the product of just one moment in history, and then passed away. In the opening years of the seventeenth century, the single broad audience of the 1590s began to split into two different audiences: a courtly audience at the more expensive indoor theatres, and a more popular audience at the old public theatres. Shakespeare's theatre, the Globe, with its great prestige, probably managed to retain a broad audience until the end of his theatrical career. But within a few years of his death, the old public theatres had sunk to crude and noisy places where simple entertainment was given for the artisan classes, while specially built indoor theatres catered for people of the highest rank and fashion. Under the influence of the rising tide of puritanism, the middle section had dropped out of the audience, leaving a plebeian audience on the one hand and an aristocratic audience on the other. Such different theatres demanded very different kinds of play, and the synthesis of popular, learned, and courtly traditions gradually disintegrated.

The Elizabethan public theatres

The public theatres for which most of Shakespeare's plays were written were small, wooden, open-air theatres, in which the plays were performed by daylight. The width of a theatre was always as great as its length: it could be round, or square, but not oblong. The Fortune Theatre was eighty feet square outside, and fifty-five feet square inside, and this was probably a typical size. A theatre consisted of three tiers of covered galleries surrounding an open central arena. From one side, the main stage projected halfway into the arena, partly protected from the weather by a roof supported at the front by two pillars. The actors came on to the stage through large doors on each side of the back wall. They were very close to the audience, which was on three sides of the stage. Some spectators stood in the arena, while others had seats in the galleries. For obvious technical reasons, there was no front curtain to the large projecting stage, so scenes began and ended simply by the entry and exit of the characters. In the back wall behind the main stage was a small inner stage concealed by curtains: here a character could hide and spy on others, or the curtains could be opened to reveal people or things hitherto concealed from the audience. Above this inner stage, at the level of the middle tier of audience galleries, was an upper stage, which could be used to represent a balcony or an upstairs window or the walls of a town. It is used in *Richard III*, when Richard appears on the leads, flanked by two clergymen; the stage direction says that he appears 'aloft' (III.7.93), that is, on the upper stage; from there he converses with Buckingham and the citizens, who are on the main stage below.

Elizabethan theatres made little use of scenery. Portable furniture, like chairs and tables, could be carried on to the stage, and sometimes a bed was pushed on; but no attempt was made to construct realistic sets. The non-naturalistic attitude to the stage-space is illustrated in *Richard III*, V.3: in this scene, two tents are erected on the stage, one for Richard and one for Richmond; members of the two armies come and go and hold conversations, obviously without seeing their opponents; the audience is expected to believe that the two tents are in fact a couple of miles apart, one in one camp and one in the other. Since the performances were in daylight, no use was made of lighting effects, and if the dramatist wished the audience to imagine that it was dark night, or brilliant sunshine, he had to achieve his effect by means of his words. On the other hand, the theatre did make considerable use of music and of sound-effects (such as

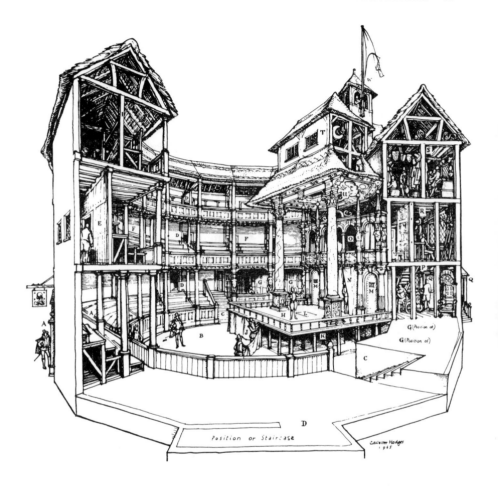

A CONJECTURAL RECONSTRUCTION OF THE INTERIOR OF
THE GLOBE PLAYHOUSE

AA Main entrance
 B The Yard
CC Entrances to lowest gallery
 D Entrance to staircase and upper galleries
 E Corridor serving the different sections of the
    middle gallery
 F Middle gallery ('Twopenny Rooms')
 G 'Gentlemen's Rooms' or Lords' Rooms'
 H The stage
 J The hanging being put up round the stage
 K The 'Hell' under the stage
 L The stage trap, leading down to the Hell
MM Stage doors

 N Curtained 'place behind the stage'
 O Gallery above the stage, used as required
    sometimes by musicians, sometimes by
    spectators, and often as part of the play
 P Back-stage area (the tiring-house)
 Q Tiring-house door
 R Dressing-rooms
 S Wardrobe and storage
 T The hut housing the machine for lowering
    enthroned gods, etc., to the stage
 U The 'Heavens'
 W Hoisting the playhouse flag

the drums and trumpets and battle-noises in *Richard III*), and of
splendid costumes (which were usually contemporary, with no attempt
at historical accuracy). Predominantly, however, the theatre depended
on the spoken word: it was a word-centred and actor-centred drama.

Because of the absence of scenery and of a front curtain, the action of
the play could flow continuously without any break between the scenes,
like a film. As the actors walked off the stage at the end of one scene,
another group of actors came in by a different door for the next one. Nor
is it necessary for a scene to take place in a clearly defined location: if the

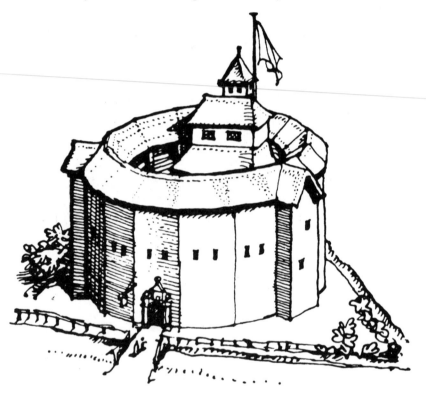

THE GLOBE PLAYHOUSE

The theatre, originally built by James Burbage in 1576, was made of wood (Burbage had been trained
as a carpenter). It was situated to the north of the River Thames on Shoreditch in Finsbury Fields.
There was trouble with the lease of the land, and so the theatre was dismantled in 1598, and recon-
structed 'in another forme' on the south side of the Thames as the Globe. Its sign is thought to have
been a figure of the Greek hero Hercules carrying the globe. It was built in six months, its galleries
being roofed with thatch. This caught fire in 1613 when some smouldering wadding, from a cannon
used in a performance of Shakespeare's *Henry VIII*, lodged in it. The theatre was burnt down, and
when it was rebuilt again on the old foundations, the galleries were roofed with tiles.

audience needs to know the location, it will be indicated by the speakers; but often there is no indication. Modern editions of the plays often give a location at the beginning of each scene (for instance, 'Act I Scene 1. London. A street'); but most of these locations have been added by modern editors, and are not found in the original editions. Time, too, may be compressed or stretched: in *Richard III*, Act V Scene 3 goes on through most of the night, but in performance the scene lasts only about twenty-five minutes.

The treatment of time and the treatment of place are to be reckoned among the conventions of the Elizabethan theatre, for all drama rests on unstated assumptions which the audience has to accept. Another convention is that characters can speak in verse, as they do almost exclusively in *Richard III*. Other common conventions are the aside and the soliloquy, both used extensively in *Richard III*. In the aside, we have to accept that a character can make a speech (or part of a speech) which is heard by the audience but not by the other characters on the stage; it is a way of revealing what a character is thinking. In the soliloquy, the character is alone on the stage, and utters his thoughts aloud for the audience to hear, as Richard does in the opening speech of *Richard III*; it is moreover one of the conventions that, in a soliloquy, the character speaks the truth and reveals himself as he really is.

The literary background

However broad the audience of the public theatre, the men who wrote the plays for it in Shakespeare's time were usually men of education. Shakespeare himself did not go to a university, but he almost certainly went to a grammar school and it is clear from his work that, while not a scholar, he was steeped in the learning of his time.

By the late sixteenth century, English education was dominated by the ideas of the humanists, ideas which had arisen in Italy in the late Middle Ages and gradually spread to northern Europe. Basically, Renaissance humanism was the belief in a certain type of education, namely one based on the pagan classics—the poetry, drama, oratory, history, and philosophy of ancient Greece and Rome. In practice it was Roman civilisation that was dominant. In Elizabethan grammar schools, the pupils were taught to read and write classical Latin, and also to speak it. They read Latin authors, with special emphasis on poetry, and were taught to analyse literary texts by the methods of classical rhetoric. Rhetoric was originally the art of oratory, or speech-making, but even in antiquity its methods and procedures had been applied to literature too, and in the Renaissance the handbooks of rhetoric were commonly regarded as handbooks for poets.

When university men began to write for the public theatres in the

1580s, this classical influence entered the popular drama. It is seen, for example, in the structure of plays, notably in the five-act pattern inherited from Roman comedy; in the free use of classical allusions, especially allusions to classical mythology (the legendary stories of gods and ancient heroes); in the taking over of stock characters from Latin dramatists; and in the influence of classical rhetoric on style.

William Shakespeare

Shakespeare was born in 1564 in Stratford-upon-Avon, a West Midland market town of about two thousand inhabitants. His father, John Shakespeare, came from a family of yeomen outside Stratford, but had moved into the town and become a glover, eventually owning his own shop. He prospered, bought property, and was elected to various civic offices; and in 1568-9 he was Bailiff, the chief civic dignitary of Stratford. We know nothing of William's boyhood, but there can be little doubt that, as the son of a prosperous citizen, he went to Stratford Grammar School, which was a good school and free for the sons of Stratford burgesses. In 1582 he married Anne Hathaway, a yeoman's daughter, by whom he had three children.

Apart from his christening, his marriage, and the birth of his children, we have no firm knowledge of Shakespeare's life until 1592, when an attack on him in a pamphlet by Robert Greene shows that he was already a dramatist of some reputation in London. His earliest plays date from about 1590, and he probably went to London and became an actor there not long before that date. For Shakespeare was not like the university men who wrote for the theatre without belonging to it: he was an actor and a professional man of the theatre, and it was on the success of a theatrical company that his fortunes were founded. His plays were doubtless a great asset to his company, but it was his position as a 'sharer' in the outstanding theatrical company of the day that made him a man of substance.

London theatrical companies were organised on a cooperative basis: a number of actors (the sharers) invested jointly in the necessary equipment (books, properties), hired a theatre, and shared the proceeds after each performance. The sharers did most of the acting themselves, but they could also hire journeymen actors, and for the women's parts they had boys, who had the status of apprentices; there were no actresses in Shakespeare's time. For legal reasons each company needed the patronage of some great nobleman, whose name it took; but in fact the companies were independent commercial organisations.

In 1594 there was a regrouping of the London theatrical companies after a severe plague, and Shakespeare and seven other actors joined forces to form a new company, the Lord Chamberlain's Men, which rapidly became the leading company of the time, with Richard Burbage as its outstanding performer. In 1599 Shakespeare was one of a consortium of investors who built the famous Globe Theatre, which became the normal home of the Lord Chamberlain's Men. In 1603, when James I came to the throne, he took the company under his own patronage, and changed its name to the King's Men. Besides enjoying enormous success with the public, the company was invited more often than any other to perform at court before the sovereign during the Christmas revels and similar festivities, and Shakespeare's plays were frequently performed on these occasions.

As, after 1594, the Lord Chamberlain's Men established themselves as London's leading company, so Shakespeare established himself as its leading playwright. In the early part of his career he wrote about two plays a year, mostly history plays and comedies, and in these he achieved a brilliant synthesis of the popular, academic, and courtly traditions. After 1600 he wrote about one play a year; these were mainly tragedies, until the very end of his career, when he wrote the so-called romances. In about 1612 he retired from the London theatre and returned to Stratford, where he already owned one of the finest houses in the town. He died in 1616.

Shakespeare's history plays

By history plays we mean ones dealing with *English* history. Shakespeare wrote ten of them, and with one exception they were written in the first ten years of his career, 1590–99. The exception is *Henry VIII*, written in collaboration with John Fletcher in about 1613. Of the nine plays from the early part of his career, one stands by itself, namely *King John*. The remaining eight plays depict one continuous period of English history from the reign of Richard II in the fourteenth century to the accession of Henry VII, the first of the Tudor kings, in 1485. These eight plays are often called Shakespeare's history cycle.

The four plays depicting the earlier events of the cycle were in fact written later than the four plays depicting the later events. *Richard II* (c. 1595) shows the deposition and murder of Richard II by his cousin Henry Bolingbroke, Duke of Lancaster, who becomes king as Henry IV. The two parts of *Henry IV* (c. 1597) show the consequent troubles of Henry IV's reign, as the noblemen who helped him to the throne rebel against him in turn. In *Henry V* (1599), these troubles for the Lancastrian monarchy are temporarily smoothed over, as Henry IV's son, the great warrior-king Henry V, leads his English army to the conquest of France. But retribution is merely postponed: in the other half of the cycle, the consequences of the original murder and deposition of Richard II come home to roost. The three parts of *Henry VI*

(c. 1590–91) begin immediately after the death of Henry V; during the long reign of his son, the English possessions in France are lost, and then civil war breaks out in England, as the Duke of York challenges the Lancastrian right to the throne. After bloody wars and murders, the Yorkists triumph, and the eldest son of the Duke of York becomes king as Edward IV. In *Richard III* (c. 1593) the youngest brother of Edward IV schemes and murders his way to the throne, and becomes Richard III, but finally this monster-king is overthrown and killed by Henry, Earl of Richmond, who unites the houses of York and Lancaster by marrying the Yorkist heiress, and inaugurates the Tudor era as Henry VII.

Henry VII had been careful to get the history of these troubles related by chroniclers from his own point of view, and the sources from which Shakespeare drew his material presented the official Tudor view of history. Inevitably, therefore, Shakespeare also presents this point of view in his cycle: the importance of legitimacy, the horrors of disorder and civil war, the role of the Tudors as the bringers of peace and prosperity. Despite this fact, the plays are probing and questioning ones, preoccupied with the problems of the public world—government, war, power, kingship—and with the relationship between public life and morality. There is a brilliant observation of men's behaviour in political situations which is blurred neither by sentimentality nor by cynicism. Whatever Shakespeare may have believed about hierarchy, he shows how in practice Richard II's belief in his own divine right cannot protect him against the folly of his political behaviour; and equally how the strong and efficient man who succeeds him, Henry IV, is unable to bring peace to the country, because of the way he had seized the throne.

Elizabethan English

The English language in Shakespeare's time differed in many ways from the English spoken today, and some of these differences are important for the student of Shakespeare. There are differences in vocabulary, in grammar, and in pronunciation, and something will be said about each of these, with illustrations from *Richard III*.

Vocabulary

Some words used by Shakespeare have since fallen out of use, and many more have changed in meaning since his time. Explanations of some of these words are given in Part 2 below. There are many such words, however, that occur more than once in the play, and to avoid repetition in Part 2 their meanings are instead given here:

advance: raise

again:	back
alarum:	call to arms, warning of danger, surprise attack
allies:	relatives, kinsfolk
an(d):	if
anon:	soon
ay:	yes
battle:	army
beholding:	beholden, indebted
boon:	something requested as a favour
Britain:	Breton, Brittany
brook:	endure, tolerate
chair:	throne
close:	hidden, secret, shut up
commit:	imprison
confound:	destroy, defeat, confuse
corse:	corpse, dead body
cousin:	relative, kinsman
dally:	trifle
dear:	grievous
defend:	forbid
degree:	rank
deny:	refuse
desert:	qualities, deservings
disgracious:	disliked, displeasing
divers:	various
ere:	before
e'er:	ever
exercise:	private worship, religious observance
factor:	agent
fain:	gladly, willingly
fall:	let fall
father:	father-in-law, step-father
fond(ly):	foolish(ly)
franked up:	shut in an enclosure and fed for fattening (like a hog)
grandam:	grandmother
halt:	limp, walk lamely
hie thee:	hurry, go quickly
indirect:	devious, crooked, dishonest
infer:	mention, allege
intelligence:	information
Jack:	man of the lower classes, ill-bred person
knot:	group, band, tumour
late:	recently

marry:	by (the Virgin) Mary (oath)
meed:	reward, wages
methinks:	it seems to me
methought(s):	it seemed to me
mew (up):	imprison (a bird in a cage)
moiety:	half
name:	rank, reputation
parlous:	dangerously clever, mischievous
peace:	be silent!
peevish:	foolish, mischievous, perverse
post:	ride fast, hasten
present(ly):	immediate(ly)
process:	narration, account
promise:	assure, tell
quick:	alive
rood:	the cross on which Christ was crucified
sennet:	ceremonial flourish on trumpets
several:	separate, divided
soft:	be quiet, wait a moment, not so fast
still:	always, continually
straight:	immediately
suddenly:	quickly
suffer:	permit, allow
tender:	be concerned about, hold dear
toy:	trifle, whim, fantastic idea
voice:	vote, opinion
want:	lack, be without
whe'er:	whether
wit:	understanding, intellect, genius
withal:	with, with it, moreover
wont:	accustomed
wot:	know(s)
Zounds:	by God's wounds (that is, those suffered by Christ at his crucifixion) (oath)

Many of these words also occur in more familiar senses: for example, *again* and *and* occur very frequently with their present-day meanings.

Pronunciation

For the student of Shakespeare's plays, the major differences in pronunciation are those that affect the rhythm of the verse. Some words had a different stress-pattern from the one used today. The following words had the main stress on the second syllable: *advertised, allies, aspect, obdurate, record* (noun), *triumph* (verb). On the other hand, *curtailed* and *extreme* were stressed on the first syllable, and so was *complete* when it occurred before a noun, as in *complete armour* (IV.4.190).

Many words could have one more stressed syllable than they have today: *adversary* could have a stress on the third syllable as well as on the first, and in that case it rhymed with *Mary*. Words ending in *-tion* could have an additional stress on the last syllable, and in that case the ending consisted of two syllables, not one, being pronounced *-si-on*. The following is an example from *Richard III*:

Now fills thy sleep with perturbations

(V.3.162)

Here the word *perturbations* has five syllables (*per-tur-ba-si-ons*), with stresses on the first, third, and fifth. Some other words could have this type of pronunciation, for instance, *ancient, Asia, Christian, patience, profession*: all these could be pronounced with one more syllable than today, and with an extra stress on the final syllable. On the other hand, all such words could equally well have the present-day style of pronunciation; so the poet could choose whichever suited his metre.

The verb-ending *-ed* was sometimes pronounced as a syllable in positions where today it is not, as in the following line:

Our bruised arms hung up for monuments

(I.1.6)

Here the *-ed* of *bruised* must be pronounced, giving the word two syllables.

Grammar

There are many small differences of grammar between Elizabethan English and present-day English, but we need consider only those that can seriously affect meaning.

In addition to the pronoun *you*, there was a second-person singular pronoun *thou* (accusative *thee*): it was possible to say either *you walk* or *thou walkest*. (In the plural, only *you* could be used.) *You* was the polite singular form, used to a social superior, or by a child to its parent; among the upper classes, it was the normal form to a social equal. *Thou* was used to a social inferior, a child, an animal; it was also the normal form used by the lower classes when addressing one another. *Thou* could also be used for emotional effect: among upper-class people on intimate terms, it marked affection or intimacy; but to a stranger it was insulting or hostile. To use *thou* to a social superior was insulting in the extreme. In *Richard III*, in the scene where Clarence is murdered (I.4), the two murderers (obviously lower-class characters) regularly address Clarence (a prince) as *you*, while he regularly replies with *thou* (except when he addresses them both together); but when the murderers become angry and excited they instead address Clarence as *thou* (ll.204–28); when they cool down, they revert to *you* (l.235). In the scene where Richard woos Anne (I.2), he addresses her with the polite *you*, but she replies with the hostile and insulting *thou*; when, however, she finally weakens, Richard switches to the intimate *thou* (ll.203–8), and she abandons her hostility and uses the polite *you* (ll.220–3). For historical reasons, it was also customary (contrary to what might be expected) to address God as *thou*; and hence it also became normal to use *thou* to a pagan god, or an abstraction, or a personified inanimate object: Rivers, for example, addresses Pomfret Castle as *thou* (III.3.8).

Today, if there is no other auxiliary in the sentence, we form questions and negatives by inserting auxiliary *do*: we turn *You know* into *Do you know?* and *You do not know*. Shakespeare also used these forms, but equally well he could say *Know you?* and *You know not*, without using *do*. Moreover, he could insert *do* in affirmative statements, and say *I do know*; and the main thing here is that the *do* is not stressed, and does not denote emphasis (as it would today). So Richard says:

> Simple plain Clarence, I do love thee so
> That I will shortly send thy soul to Heaven
>
> (I.1.118–19)

Here, *I do love* is merely another way of saying *I love*, and must be read with the word *do* quite unstressed.

In verbs, there were two alternative endings for the third-person singular in the present tense, *-(e)th* and *-(e)s*, as in *he walks* and *he walketh*; in Shakespeare's time, the *-(e)s* forms were normal in speech, while the *-(e)th* forms were rather literary and formal. In the present-tense plural, the form with no ending was normal, like *they walk*; but it was also possible to use forms like *they walks* and *they walketh*. These occur occasionally in Shakespeare. An example of the *-(e)s* plural is:

> Untimely storms makes men expect a dearth
>
> (II.3.35)

In the second and third person singular of the present tense, the subjunctive was still commonly used: alongside *he walks* (or *walketh*) and *thou walkest* we find the subjunctive forms *he walk* and *thou walk*. In subordinate clauses, the use of the subjunctive indicated doubt, uncertainty, unreality; it was therefore very common in *if*-clauses, like the following:

> What if it come to thee again?
>
> (I.4.135)

In main clauses, the subjunctive is used to express a wish, as in the following:

> Edward thy son, that now is Prince of Wales,
> For Edward our dear son, that was Prince of Wales,
> Die in his youth by like untimely violence!
> Thyself a queen, for me that was a queen,
> Outlive thy glory, like my wretched self!
>
> (I.3.198–202)

This means 'May Edward die ... mayst thou outlive thy glory'.

Today, the relative pronouns *which* and *who* are chosen according to whether they refer to a person or not; but in Elizabethan English it was quite normal to use *which* for persons, as in the following example:

> With that sour ferryman which poets write of
>
> (I.4.46)

In the sixteenth century, the word *its* did not exist; the possessive form of *it* was *his*, as in:

> Thy crown, usurped, disgraced his kingly glory
>
> (IV.4.371)

The use of *his*, therefore, does not imply personification.

A note on the text

In 1623, seven years after Shakespeare's death, some of his former colleagues published his collected plays in one large volume. This was a folio volume; that is, the pages were very large, since each consisted of half a sheet of paper: each sheet was folded only once in the making of the book. This edition of 1623 is called the Shakespeare First Folio (F1 for short), and is our sole authority for about half the plays. A number of plays, however, had been published in his lifetime, as quarto volumes. A quarto is smaller than a folio, since each page represents only a quarter of a sheet of paper: each sheet is folded twice in the making of the book.

The first edition of *Richard III* was a quarto (Q1) published in 1597. The play was obviously very popular, for five further quarto editions (Q2–Q6) followed in the succeeding twenty-five years. Each of these quartos was printed from the previous one, with the addition of further mistakes each time, so the later quartos have no authority. Q1 was probably a text constructed from memory by the actors when they were on a provincial tour, and used as a prompt copy. It is a shortened version of the play, for 200 lines are missing which appear in F1. The F1 version was probably printed from a copy of Q3 which had been corrected from Shakespeare's manuscript and used in the theatre as a prompt copy.

Modern editors tend to follow F1, which seems to offer the most authentic text; but there is a case for some readings from Q1; and there are forty lines of text in Q1 which are missing from F1.

In Q1 the play is not divided into acts and the scenes are not numbered. In F1 the play is divided into five acts, and the scenes are numbered, but there is an obvious mistake in the act divisions, which is normally corrected by modern editors.

Different editions of *Richard III* will be found to have slightly different line numbers. It is therefore necessary to give line numbers from one particular edition, and for these notes the edition chosen is a cheap and easily available paperback, in the New Penguin Shakespeare series: *King Richard III*, edited by E.A.J. Honigmann, Penguin Books, Harmondsworth, 1968. If you use a different edition, you should have no difficulty in identifying passages referred to, since the numbering is seldom likely to differ by more than a few lines.

Part 2

Summaries

of RICHARD III

A general summary

In the civil wars between the houses of York and Lancaster (the Wars of the Roses), the Yorkists have triumphed, and Edward Duke of York has become king as Edward IV. The Lancastrian king, Henry VI, is dead, and so is his son Edward, Prince of Wales, both murdered by Richard Duke of Gloucester, youngest brother of Edward IV. Richard now plans to obtain the crown for himself, but there are many obstacles: Edward IV is dying, but he has two young sons; he also has another brother, George Duke of Clarence, who has a son and a daughter; all these are nearer in succession to the throne than Richard. Richard acts the part of a simple, honest man, but secretly schemes against those who stand between him and the throne. He contrives to have Clarence imprisoned in the Tower of London by the king, and then has him murdered there. He persuades Anne, widow of the Lancastrian Prince of Wales, to marry him. At court, he stirs up dissension between the older nobility and the relatives of Edward IV's queen, Elizabeth, who has come from a relatively humble family.

While the nobility are squabbling, Queen Margaret, widow of Henry VI, enters and curses them all for their crimes against the Lancastrians during the civil wars, and prophesies their destruction; in the course of the play, her prophecies come true. King Edward dies, and his elder son, Prince Edward, is proclaimed king; but he is still a child, and Richard is Lord Protector, and so has effective power. The Duke of Buckingham becomes Richard's confidant, and supports him in his plans to become king. A party of noblemen rides to Ludlow to bring Prince Edward to London for his coronation; on the way, Richard and Buckingham arrest three of Queen Elizabeth's powerful relatives, and have them executed. When Prince Edward comes to London, he and his younger brother are lodged in the Tower. Richard sounds out the Lord Chamberlain, Hastings, to see if he can gain his support, but Hastings is faithful to Prince Edward; Richard invents a pretext to have Hastings arrested as a traitor and executed. Buckingham addresses the citizens of London, arguing that the sons of Edward IV are illegitimate, and that Richard should be king; the citizens show no enthusiasm, but nevertheless a deputation led by the Lord Mayor visits Richard and calls on him to become king; after several pretended refusals, Richard allows himself to be persuaded, and accepts the crown. He is crowned king as Richard III, and his wife Anne as queen.

Richard wishes to murder the two princes in the Tower, and consults Buckingham, who hesitates; in response, Richard refuses to give Buckingham the reward he had promised for his support; Buckingham flees to Wales and raises an army. Richard has the two princes murdered in the Tower. He also has his wife Anne murdered, for he has decided that it is politically necessary for him to marry his niece Elizabeth, daughter of Edward IV. Queen Margaret gloats over the disasters that have befallen her enemies. Richard leads an army against Buckingham; he is intercepted by Queen Elizabeth and his mother, the Duchess of York, who revile him for his crimes; Richard tries to persuade Queen Elizabeth to woo her daughter Elizabeth on his behalf; after a long argument, she appears to agree. Buckingham's army is dispersed by floods, and he himself is captured and executed. Henry Earl of Richmond, who has a claim to the throne through the Lancastrian line, lands with an army in South Wales, and is joined by many gentlemen who are discontented with Richard. The powerful Lord Stanley (Earl of Derby) is step-father to Richmond, and Richard does not trust him; Stanley's forces join Richard's army, but Richard holds Stanley's son George as a hostage, to make sure of his loyalty. Queen Elizabeth secretly lets Richmond know that she agrees to a marriage between him and her daughter Elizabeth.

The armies of Richard and Richmond meet near Market Bosworth. The evening before the battle, Stanley secretly visits Richmond and promises to give him as much help as he safely can. During the night, while Richard and Richmond are sleeping, they are visited in dreams by the ghosts of all those that Richard had murdered, who encourage Richmond but threaten Richard, telling him to despair and die. When the battle begins, Stanley refuses to bring his forces in on Richard's side; but it is too late for Richard to execute George Stanley. In the battle, Richard performs heroically, but is defeated and killed. The crown is taken from his head and given to Richmond (Henry VII), who promises to marry Princess Elizabeth, thus uniting the warring houses of York and Lancaster. He prays that, as a result of this union, civil war may end, and England have peace and prosperity.

Detailed summaries

Act I Scene 1

In a soliloquy, Richard Duke of Gloucester tells us that the civil wars have ended, and people are now enjoying the pleasures of peace under a Yorkist king. Richard, however, takes no pleasure in love or peaceful pursuits, and has decided to be a villain. He has caused dissension between his two brothers, the King and Clarence, and Clarence is about to be imprisoned. Clarence enters under armed guard, on his way to the Tower. Richard pretends to sympathise with him, and suggests that it is the Queen and her relatives who have caused his imprisonment; he himself will do everything in his power to get Clarence released. Clarence goes, and Lord Hastings enters, just released from imprisonment; he tells Richard that the King is extremely ill, and his physicians fear for his life. In a final soliloquy, Richard reveals his plans to have Clarence killed before the King dies, and to marry the Lady Anne.

NOTES AND GLOSSARY:

winter:	the civil wars between the houses of York and Lancaster
sun of York:	Edward IV, who has become king after the defeat of the Lancastrians by the Yorkists. The sun was an emblem of kingship, and was also one of the badges used by the Yorkists. There is a pun on 'son': Edward was the son of Richard Duke of York, killed by the Lancastrians in 1460
measures:	stately dances; tunes, melodies
front:	forehead
barbed:	protected by armour
But I that am not shaped ...:	Richard is physically deformed; he has a hump on his back, as the play frequently reminds us
rudely stamped:	imperfectly shaped, like a coin which has not been properly minted
piping:	accompanied by the music of pipes (woodwind instruments). The peaceful world which Richard despises is characterised by music (*lute, piping*), dancing (*measures, capers, strut*), and love-making (*lady's chamber, lascivious, amorous, wanton*)
descant:	comment
inductions:	preparations, first steps
say that G:	Clarence's name was George. But Richard's own title (Gloucester) begins with the same letter
the Tower:	the Tower of London, a royal castle. It was often used for the imprisonment of people of high rank who were charged with treason or other serious crimes
godfathers:	sponsors at a child's baptism into the Christian Church, who give him his Christian names and guarantee his religious education
cross-row:	alphabet

Lady Grey: Edward IV's queen had been the widow of a poor knight, Sir John Grey. The marriage caused offence to the nobility, who resented the advancement given to Elizabeth's relatives, the Woodvilles

tempers him to this extremity: moulds him (like wax) so that he behaves with this extreme severity

Anthony Woodville: Earl Rivers, brother to Queen Elizabeth

Mistress Shore: Jane Shore, wife of a London citizen. She was the mistress of Edward IV, and then of Hastings

my Lord Chamberlain: Hastings

The jealous ... and herself: the Queen and Jane Shore

gossips: friends, cronies

straitly: strictly

have naught ... doth naught: Brakenbury uses *naught* in the sense of 'nothing', but Richard deliberately misunderstands him, and uses *naught* in the sense of 'wickedness, immoral act'

abjects: outcasts, people who are cast off or rejected. Richard uses the word sarcastically instead of 'subjects'

lie for you: (a) lie in prison, (b) tell lies. Clarence understands only the first meaning

kites and buzzards: two birds of prey of the falcon family; *kite* also meant 'person who preys on others, swindler', and *buzzard* meant 'stupid, worthless, or ignorant person'. The eagle, on the other hand, was regarded as the symbol of nobility or royalty

fear him: fear for his life

diet: way of life

with post-horse: at great speed

Warwick's youngest daughter: Anne Neville, widow of Edward Prince of Wales (son of Henry VI). She was a daughter of the powerful Earl of Warwick, the so-called 'kingmaker'

run before my horse to market: count my chickens before they are hatched (proverbial)

Act I Scene 2

The body of Henry VI is being carried to burial, with Lady Anne following it as mourner. She laments the death of the king, and of his son, her late husband; and she curses Richard, who had murdered them both. Richard enters, and woos Anne; at first she is violently hostile, but in the end his powers of persuasion win her over. In a final soliloquy,

Richard exults at his own brilliant skill in winning her, and suggests ironically that he must be a handsome man after all.

NOTES AND GLOSSARY:

halberds: men armed with halberds. The halberd was a combination of a spear and battle-axe, mounted on a long handle

obsequiously: dutifully

virtuous Lancaster: Henry VI, who was a Lancastrian king

invocate: call on

these windows: Henry's wounds

the helpless balm ... eyes: her tears, which have no power to soothe or heal

More direful hap betide: may a more terrible fate fall upon

Prodigious: abnormal, monstrous

Chertsey: a monastery about twenty miles from London

Paul's: St Paul's Cathedral in London

Avaunt: go away

curst: angry, shrewish, cantankerous

pattern: example

Dead Henry's wounds ... afresh: there was a common superstition that the wounds of a murdered man began bleeding again in the presence of his murderer

By circumstance: by a detailed account

current: acceptable

falchion: a broad, slightly curved sword

holp: helped

timeless: untimely, premature

Plantagenets: Plantagenet was the surname of the English royal family from 1154 to 1485. The houses of both York and Lancaster were Plantagenets (see l.142 below, where Richard refers to himself as Plantagenet)

rent: rend, tear

wrack: injury, destruction

basilisks: fabulous reptiles, which could kill by a look

These eyes, which never shed ... sword at him: after the Lancastrian victory at the Battle of Wakefield in 1460, the Duke of York's son, Edmund Earl of Rutland, was murdered by Lord Clifford. Shakespeare had depicted the incident in 3 *Henry VI*

thy warlike father: Richard Neville, Earl of Warwick (1428–71). He supported the Yorkist cause, and played a large part in its success. In 1469, however, he quarrelled with Edward IV, and went over to the Lancastrians; it was then that his daughter Anne was married to the Lancastrian Prince of Wales. For a time Warwick was able to restore Henry VI to the throne, but in 1471 he was defeated by Edward IV at Barnet, and was killed in the battle

my father's death: after the Battle of Wakefield (1460), the Duke of York was captured by the Lancastrians, crowned with a paper crown, taunted, and then murdered

All men, I hope, live so: because they live in hope of salvation through Christ

To take is not to give: Anne accepts the ring, but promises nothing in return. Nevertheless, the acceptance of the ring shows clearly that Richard has won her

Crosby House: a large house in Bishopsgate Street in London, one of Richard's residences

expedient: speedy

Whitefriars: a priory (monastery) of the Carmelites (white friars) in Fleet Street, outside the walls of the city to the west

bleeding witness: the body of Henry VI

Tewkesbury: in 1471, a few weeks after Warwick's defeat at Barnet, Queen Margaret and Prince Edward were defeated by the Yorkists at Tewkesbury, and Edward was killed. In Shakespeare's version of the event, in *3 Henry VI*, Prince Edward is stabbed in turn by Edward IV, Richard, and Clarence

denier: a French copper coin of very small value

marvellous proper: wonderfully handsome

Act I Scene 3

Queen Elizabeth is distressed and apprehensive because of the illness of her husband; she is comforted by her relatives. Stanley (Derby) and Buckingham report that the King is cheerful, and wishes to reconcile the quarrelling factions in his court. Richard enters, and begins an altercation with the Queen and her relatives. Queen Margaret comes in and listens unseen, commenting caustically on what they say. Finally she comes forward and denounces them; they in turn denounce her for her cruelty; she curses them all, and prophesies their destruction. Queen Elizabeth and the courtiers are summoned to the King. Richard soliloquises on his cleverness in stirring up mischief. Two murderers come to him, and he gives them a warrant for the execution of Clarence.

NOTES AND GLOSSARY:

Dorset ... Grey: Queen Elizabeth's sons by her first marriage

Protector: the regent who governed the kingdom while the King was under age

determined, not concluded: decided, but not formally enacted

The Countess Richmond: Margaret Beaufort, widow of Edmund Tudor, Earl of Richmond; their son is the Lancastrian claimant to the throne who, at the end of the play, defeats Richard III and becomes Henry VII. After the death of Edmund Tudor, she married Thomas Lord Stanley, who later became Earl of Derby

cog: deceive, fawn, wheedle

apish: affected, fantastically foolish

The King ... makes him to send: this sentence is confused: the word *King* is not followed by any suitable verb. The meaning, however, is plain enough

Aiming: guessing

Our brother: Clarence

ennoble: raise to the ranks of the nobility

noble: a coin worth six shillings and eightpence

suspects: suspicions

marry ... marry: Richard first uses the word as a mild oath, and then puns on the meaning 'to enter into marriage'

Iwis: certainly, assuredly

Queen Margaret: Margaret of Anjou, widow of Henry VI

packhorse: drudge, one who works hard without much reward

factious for: on the side of

husband ... Saint Albans: Queen Elizabeth's first husband, Sir John Grey, was killed at the Battle of St Albans (1461), fighting on the Lancastrian side

his father, Warwick: in 1469 Clarence married Warwick's elder daughter, Isabel, and in 1470 he helped Warwick to drive out Edward IV and restore Henry VI; but when Edward IV invaded England in 1471, Clarence went over to his side again and helped him to defeat Warwick and the Lancastrians

cacodemon: evil spirit

pilled: plundered, taken by force

repetition: narration, statement

clout: cloth

Northumberland: the Earl of Northumberland fought on the Lancastrian side at the Battle of Wakefield. In Shakespeare's *3 Henry VI*, he weeps for pity when Clifford and Queen Margaret taunt the captured Duke of York and give him a cloth dipped in the blood of his son Rutland

stalled:	installed
charm:	magic spell, incantation
hag:	witch
elvish-marked:	marked at birth by evil fairies
abortive:	born prematurely
rag of honour:	contemptible and defective member of a noble family
bottled:	shaped like a bottle, swollen
false-boding:	prophesying falsely
do me duty:	treat me with the deference due to a queen
malapert:	impudent, cheeky. Dorset is young, and Margaret puts him firmly in his place
Your fire-new ... current:	Dorset's recently acquired title (*honour*) is compared to the design stamped on a coin which is fresh from the mint (*fire-new*) and not yet in circulation (*scarce current*)
aery:	eagle's nest, and the young eagles in it (the House of York)
My charity is outrage:	the only charity shown to me is violent injury
Look when:	whenever
rankle:	cause a festering wound
soothe:	flatter
set abroach:	pierce a cask and leave the liquor running out; hence, set afoot, diffuse
odd old ends:	miscellaneous old fragments
Crosby Place:	another name for Crosby House (see I.2.112)
eyes drop millstones:	a proverbial expression, used of hard-hearted people

---

Act I Scene 4

Clarence, imprisoned in the Tower, tells his gaoler of a terrifying dream he has had. He dreamed that he escaped from the Tower and took ship with his brother Gloucester, who accidentally knocked him overboard; he drowned in great pain; his soul went to the underworld, where he was reproached for his crimes of perjury and murder, and attacked by a host of Furies, whereupon he woke. Clarence goes to sleep. The two Murderers come with their warrant, and are left alone with him. They wake him, and he pleads for his life. After a long argument, one of the murderers relents, but the other kills Clarence and drags his body off.

NOTES AND GLOSSARY:

Keeper:	gaoler. In the quarto texts, this is the same person as Brakenbury, the Lieutenant of the Tower; but in the

Burgundy: First Folio, the Keeper and Brakenbury are two separate persons, the latter not entering until l.75 at that time a large duchy, including the Netherlands. Clarence's sister Margaret was married to the Duke of Burgundy

hatches: deck (of moveable planks)

yield the ghost: die

my panting bulk, Who: the panting body of me, who. The word *who* refers to *my*, not to *bulk*

melancholy flood ... ferryman: in classical mythology, the souls of the dead had to cross the Styx, a river of the underworld, in order to reach Tartarus, the land of the dead. They were ferried across the Styx by the miserly Charon, in a small boat

perjury: Clarence broke an oath when, in 1471, he abandoned Warwick and Henry VI and returned to the camp of Edward IV

shadow like an angel: this is the spirit of Edward, the Lancastrian Prince of Wales

requits: repays, rewards

for unfelt imaginations: in place of the things which they are believed to have but which in fact they do not experience

Judgement Day: the end of the world, when the dead will rise and God sit in judgement on all men

passionate humour: compassionate mood

tells: counts

entertain: keep in their service, employ

tall: brave, good at fighting

malmsey-butt: barrel of wine. Malmsey was a strong, sweet wine from Greece

sop: piece of bread dipped in water or wine

quest: jury

convict: convicted

King of kings: God

table of his law: a reference to the biblical Ten Commandments. The sixth is 'Thou shalt not kill' (Exodus 20:13)

receive the sacrament: take a solemn religious oath

bloody minister: executioner

gallant-springing: growing up in beauty, or in courage and chivalry

brave Plantagenet: Prince Edward of Lancaster

deceived: mistaken

lessoned: taught

he is kind: Clarence means 'affectionate, tender', but the Murderer plays on the other meaning, 'natural'

like Pilate: Pontius Pilate, the Roman procurator (governor) of Palestine at the time of the crucifixion of Christ. According to the biblical account, Pilate did not wish to crucify Christ, but gave way to pressure from the Jews; he then publicly washed his hands in water, and disclaimed responsibility for the crucifixion (Matthew 27:11–25)

By heaven the Duke shall know how slack you have been: this is the reading of F1, and is followed by many editors, but is almost certainly wrong, because (a) it is impossible as a line of blank verse, and (b) the Murderer addresses his fellow-murderer as *you*, for which there is no conceivable motivation. Lower-class characters regularly addressed one another (in the singular) as 'thou'. In this scene, the murderers invariably say *thou* to one another, except in this one line. The reading of Q1 is *By heavens the Duke shall know how slack thou art*. This is a perfect line of blank verse, and uses the correct pronoun, *thou*.

Act II Scene 1

Edward IV, near to death, has reconciled the warring factions at his court, at least in appearance; the various lords swear their friendship for one another, and for the Queen. Richard enters, and similarly protests his amity for everybody. The Queen asks the King to be reconciled to Clarence; at this Richard pretends to take offence: the Queen is insulting him, since everybody knows that Clarence is dead. The King and the court are shocked: this is the first knowledge they have of Clarence's death. Stanley (Derby) enters, and asks the King's pardon for one of his followers who has killed a man in a brawl. In a speech of grief and reproach, the King asks why nobody had reminded him of all the services that Clarence had done him in the past; nobody spoke up for him, but when one of their menials has committed a drunken murder they immediately come to the King for pardon. The King is helped away to his private apartment in a state of near-collapse. Richard suggests that the death of Clarence has been contrived by the relatives of the Queen.

NOTES AND GLOSSARY:

I every day expect ... hence: ·he expects to die. An *embassage* is a message from an ambassador (here, death); the *Redeemer* is Christ

period: completion

swelling:	full of pride, arrogant
heap:	large company
hardly borne:	taken amiss, resented
all without desert:	completely without my deserving it
compounded:	settled
presence:	presence-chamber (king's reception-room)
Mercury:	the Roman god Mercury was the messenger of the gods, depicted as a young man with winged sandals and a winged hat
lag:	late
go current from:	are free from
forfeit ... servant's life:	my servant's life, which will otherwise be forfeited
lap:	cover, wrap
thin:	thinly covered
Sinfully:	in traditional Christian thought, Wrath (anger) is one of the seven deadly sins (the most serious sins, which cause spiritual death)
The precious image ... Redeemer:	a man. According to the Bible, God created man in his own image (Genesis 1:26)
closet:	private apartment (in contrast to the presence-chamber, where the King gave audiences)

Act II Scene 2

The two children of Clarence question their grandmother, the old Duchess of York, about their father's death; they believe Richard's version of events. The Queen enters with the news that the King has died; she and the duchess lament. Richard and the principal nobles come in; Buckingham proposes that a small party should be sent to Ludlow to fetch the young Edward Prince of Wales (elder son of Edward IV) to London to be crowned king. Rivers asks why it should be a small party; Buckingham persuades him that this is necessary. They go off to hold a council to decide who shall go to Ludlow. From a private interchange between Richard and Buckingham, we learn that they are planning to separate the Queen's relatives from the young prince.

NOTES AND GLOSSARY:

Duchess of York:	the widow of Richard Duke of York, and mother of Edward IV, Clarence, and Richard
Incapable:	lacking the power of understanding
impeachments:	accusations
visor:	mask, disguise
interest:	right to a share in (a legal term)

title:	legal rights
his images:	his sons
two mirrors:	Edward IV and Clarence. When she looks at them, she sees the qualities of their father
false glass:	Richard, who does not resemble his father
reduce:	bring back. Her eyes are like the sea, into which all streams (*springs*) flow back
watery:	having influence on the sea. The moon causes the tides
parcelled:	divided into small portions, particular
opposite with:	opposed to the will of
butt-end:	the thicker end of anything; hence, the better concluding part
cloudy:	sad, full of foreboding
Me seemeth:	it seems to me
Ludlow:	a town and castle in Shropshire, about 140 miles north-west of London. At the time of Edward IV's death, Prince Edward and his household were living there
estate is green:	state (kingdom) is unripe (weak, unseasoned)
sort occasion:	find an opportunity
index:	preface, prologue. This speech is the first clear sign of Buckingham's alliance with Richard. The *story* is presumably their scenario for Richard's attempt on the crown
consistory:	council chamber. Richard flatters Buckingham by suggesting that all the good ideas come from him, while Richard merely follows

---

Act II Scene 3

Three citizens discuss the state of the realm following the death of Edward IV. The First Citizen is optimistic, the Second is doubtful, the Third is full of fear and foreboding: it is unfavourable for a country to be governed by a child; and there are dangerous factions at court, which need to be ruled, not to rule.

NOTES AND GLOSSARY:

by'r Lady:	by Our Lady (the Virgin Mary, mother of Christ). A petty oath
seldom comes the better:	change is usually for the worse (proverbial)
giddy:	changeable, unstable, mad
God speed:	may God make you succeed (prosper). A conventional greeting

hold: hold good, prove to be true
Woe to that land ... child: echoing the Bible: 'Woe to thee, O land, when thy king is a child' (Ecclesiastes 10:16)
In him there is ... govern well: under him (Prince Edward) there is hope of (good) government: while he is a child, his council will govern well; when he is mature, he himself will
solace: take comfort, have enjoyment
sort: ordains, orders
mistrust: expect, fear
proof: experience

Act II Scene 4

The Archbishop of York, the young Duke of York, Queen Elizabeth, and the Duchess of York look forward to the coming of Prince Edward, who is on his way to London from Ludlow. Young York makes witty comments about his uncle Richard, and is rebuked by his mother for such dangerous talk. A messenger reports that Rivers, Grey, and Vaughan have been arrested by Richard and Buckingham, and imprisoned in Pomfret Castle. Queen Elizabeth sees that the ruin of her family is imminent, and decides to go into sanctuary with young York; the Duchess of York accompanies her.

NOTES AND GLOSSARY:
young Duke of York: Richard, younger son of Edward IV and Elizabeth, then aged ten
Stony Stratford: a small town in Buckinghamshire, about fifty miles north-west of London
Northampton: a large town fourteen miles north of Stony Stratford. The curious route was part of the manoeuvre by Richard and Buckingham whereby they split the party into two, to facilitate the arrest of the Woodvilles
the Prince: Edward Prince of Wales, elder son of Edward IV and Elizabeth. At the time of his father's death he was thirteen years old
Small herbs ... apace: proverbial
fast ... haste: a rhyme, depending on the pronunciation of both words with a short 'a'
Pitchers have ears: there is a proverb *Little pitchers have long ears*, meaning 'children hear more things than people imagine'. But Elizabeth perhaps means 'There may be listeners anywhere: you have to be careful what you say'. The *ears* of a pitcher are its handles

Pomfret:	Pontefract, a town and castle in Yorkshire
Vaughan:	a high ranking royal official, at that time chamberlain to Prince Edward. He was a supporter of the Woodville faction. His name was probably pronounced as two syllables (not one, as today)
jut:	encroach. The quartos read *jet*, with the same meaning
aweless:	not inspiring awe
seated:	established in power
preposterous:	contrary to the order of nature
outrage:	violence, violent behaviour
spleen:	ill nature, malice
sanctuary:	a holy place (usually a church) where fugitives were immune from arrest. Elizabeth, who was in the Palace of Westminster, took refuge in the nearby sanctuary in Westminster Abbey
seal:	the Great Seal of England, used to authenticate all important royal documents. It was kept by the Lord Chancellor; in 1483 the Archbishop of York was Chancellor

Act III Scene 1

Prince Edward enters London with Richard and Buckingham. He expresses his displeasure at the arrest of his mother's relatives. Hastings reports that Queen Elizabeth and York have taken sanctuary. Buckingham asks Cardinal Bourchier to persuade Elizabeth to send York to them; if she refuses, Hastings is to bring him by force; Buckingham persuades the cardinal that this would not be a breach of sanctuary. Richard tells the prince that he is to stay in the Tower for a few days. Hastings and Bourchier return with York, who exercises his wit on Richard. The two young princes go off to the Tower. Richard and Buckingham send Catesby to sound out Hastings, to see if he will support Richard's bid for the crown. Richard tells Buckingham that, if Hastings will not support them, they will have him executed. He promises Buckingham the earldom of Hereford as his reward for helping him to the throne.

NOTES AND GLOSSARY:

Lord Cardinal:	Thomas Bourchier, Archbishop of Canterbury
your chamber:	London, which was called the Chamber of the Kings of England. Richard and Buckingham have been travelling with the prince, and they are congratulating him on his arrival in his capital

crosses: vexations, troubles. He is referring to the arrest of the Woodvilles, as can be seen from his wish (l.6) for more uncles to welcome him

jumpeth: coincides, agrees

slug: slow fellow, sluggard

will our mother come?: Prince Edward sometimes uses the royal plural, referring to himself as 'we' instead of 'I', especially when speaking formally (see ll.61, 96, 98). When speaking less formally he says 'I' (see ll.68–93)

perforce: forcibly, by force

ceremonious: punctilious, scrupulous about forms

Weigh it but ... age: if you judge it by the coarse standards of our times

Julius Caesar: a famous Roman general and statesman (*c.* 101–44BC). On two occasions he mounted small-scale invasions of Britain. It was popularly believed that he had begun the building of the Tower of London, but in fact the oldest part of the Tower dates from about AD1080

re-edified: rebuilt

the general all-ending day: the Last Judgement, the end of the world

characters: letters, writing

the formal Vice, Iniquity: the Vice, sometimes called Iniquity, was a stock character of the old morality plays; *formal* means 'normal, regular'

moralize: interpret, explain

our ancient right in France: from 1340 onwards, the kings of England claimed that they were the rightful heirs to the throne of France, and made many attempts to enforce their claim. The zenith of English power in France was achieved by Henry V, whose son Henry VI was in 1422 crowned king of England and of France; but in the course of Henry VI's reign, the English were driven out of France, except for Calais

lightly: commonly, often

light gifts: punning on the meaning 'unimportant, trivial'

I weigh it ... heavier: I think it unimportant, even if it were heavier

like an ape: apes or monkeys were often led or carried about for show, and sometimes sat on a saddle on their keeper's shoulder. York is referring (not very tactfully) to Richard's humped back

sharp-provided: keen and ready

seat royal: throne

complots: plots

look when: as soon as

betimes:	early
digest:	consider, think over, arrange (with a pun on the digestion of food)
form:	good order

Act III Scene 2

A messenger from Stanley comes to Hastings, suggesting that they should immediately ride away to the north together, because there is danger from Richard. Stanley has had an ominous dream, and he distrusts Richard's plan to hold two separate councils. Hastings dismisses these fears as groundless; he sends the messenger back to Stanley, urging him to come to Hastings so that they can go together to the meeting of the council, which is in the Tower. Catesby brings Hastings the news that his old enemies, the Queen's relatives, are to be executed that day at Pomfret; he asks Hastings whether he would support an attempt by Richard to become king; Hastings refuses flatly. Stanley comes, and repeats his fears, but agrees to accompany Hastings to the Tower.

NOTES AND GLOSSARY:

the boar:	Richard, whose badge was a white boar
razed off his helm:	torn off his helmet
without instance:	needless, without cause
they account his head upon the Bridge:	they regard him as already dead. The heads of executed traitors were displayed on poles on London Bridge
Pursuivant:	a royal messenger with power to make arrests. The meeting with the Pursuivant gives further scope for the expression of Hastings's blind over-confidence
suggestions:	incitement, false accusation
gramercy:	thank you
Sir John:	the title 'sir' was often given to priests. The meeting with the priest gives occasion for Buckingham's ironical remarks about shrift and execution
content:	pay, reward
shriving work:	shrift (confession and absolution). In the Catholic Church, the faithful periodically confess their sins to a priest, who imposes penance on them and gives them absolution from their sins. It was customary for condemned persons to be given shrift before being executed
And supper too:	Hastings is not going to leave the Tower at all: the plans for his execution have already been made

Act III Scene 3

Rivers, Grey, and Vaughan are being led to execution at Pomfret. Rivers recalls that Richard II had been murdered in this same castle. Rivers and Grey remember Margaret's curse, and pray that it may come true for others as well as for themselves.

NOTES AND GLOSSARY:
limit: prescribed period
Richard the Second: Richard II was murdered in Pomfret Castle in 1400, after being deposed by his cousin Henry, Duke of Lancaster, who became Henry IV. This act of usurpation was the origin of the civil wars between the houses of York and Lancaster
expiate: fully come

Act III Scene 4

The council is meeting to decide on the day of Prince Edward's coronation. Richard has not yet arrived, and Hastings takes the lead in the discussions. Richard enters, and privately informs Buckingham of Hastings's opposition to their aims; the two of them go off. Hastings expresses the opinion that Richard is in a good mood, and not displeased with any of them. Richard and Buckingham return, and Richard accuses Queen Elizabeth and Mistress Shore of having practised witchcraft against him; Hastings begins to speak, but Richard immediately accuses him of being a traitor, and orders his instant execution. Richard and Buckingham go off, followed by the other members of the council. Hastings laments his own folly, and prophesies misery for England; he is led off to execution.

NOTES AND GLOSSARY:
happy: favourable, suitable
Holborn: a district in the west of London. Ely House, belonging to the bishops of Ely, was in Holborn
prolonged: postponed, delayed
conceit: idea, thought
likes: pleases
livelihood: liveliness. But the quartos read *likelihood*, which may be right
blasted: infected, withered
protector of this ... strumpet: Jane Shore was Hastings's mistress, as Richard well knew (see III.1.185 above). Hastings walks straight into Richard's trap

The rest ... follow me: nobody on the council dare do other than follow Richard out, leaving Hastings to his fate

footcloth horse: horse wearing a footcloth, which was a large ornamented cloth thrown over the back of a horse and hanging down to the ground on each side

block: the piece of wood on which the condemned man placed his neck when he was beheaded

Act III Scene 5

Richard and Buckingham, still in the Tower, dress up in old armour and pretend great fear, to convince the Lord Mayor of London that there has been a plot against their lives, and so to justify the execution of Hastings without trial. The Lord Mayor agrees to explain this to the citizens. Richard sends Buckingham to address the assembled citizens, to persuade them of Richard's right to the crown.

NOTES AND GLOSSARY:

marvellous ill-favoured: having an extremely bad appearance

daubed: covered (as a wall is covered with a layer of plaster or clay)

apparent: obvious, plain

conversation: sexual relationship

from all attainder of suspects: free from all stain of suspicion

covert'st sheltered: most secret and hidden

Turks or infidels: it was commonly believed that Turkish rulers were tyrants, who executed people without trial

fair befall you: may you have good fortune

these our friends: Lovel and Ratcliffe

Something against our meaning: somewhat against our intentions

Misconster us in him: misinterpret what we have done to him

Guildhall: a building in Gresham Street, the official meeting-place of the London citizens

house: shop (not necessarily a tavern, since all kinds of shops had signs)

luxury: lust, lechery

listed: desired, wished

Baynard's Castle: one of Richard's residences, near Blackfriars

Shaw ... Penker: two doctors of divinity, famous as preachers, and supporters of Richard

take some privy order: make some secret arrangement

Act III Scene 6

In a soliloquy, a Scrivener reveals that he has copied out the indictment of Hastings, and that it was given him to do many hours before Hastings was accused.

NOTES AND GLOSSARY:

Scrivener:	scribe, professional copyist
set hand:	the style of handwriting used for official documents
engrossed:	written out in large letters
Paul's:	St Paul's Cathedral, where proclamations were often read
precedent:	previous draft
Untainted:	unaccused
gross:	dull, stupid

Act III Scene 7

Buckingham tells Richard that he has addressed the citizens, pressing Richard's claim to the throne, but they have been unresponsive. Nevertheless, the Lord Mayor and Aldermen have come to persuade him to be king. Richard pretends to be at religious devotions, and reluctant to be interrupted. Finally, he agrees to hear the deputation, and Buckingham urges him to become king. Twice Richard refuses, but finally allows himself to be persuaded, and is hailed as King Richard.

NOTES AND GLOSSARY:

Lady Lucy:	there was an allegation that, before Edward IV married Lady Grey (Queen Elizabeth), he had been betrothed to Lady Elizabeth Lucy. If this were true, his marriage with Lady Grey would be invalid, and the children of the marriage would be illegitimate, and so unable to inherit the crown
contract ... in France:	when Edward IV married Lady Grey, he was negotiating with the King of France about a marriage to the Lady Bona, sister of the French queen. He was not, however, betrothed to her, as Buckingham asserts
enforcement:	violation, rape
right idea:	exact image
victories in Scotland:	Richard commanded the English army that in 1482 invaded Scotland and captured Edinburgh
Recorder:	the Recorder of London, a magistrate appointed by the aldermen

mighty suit: great entreaty

ground ... descant: musical terms: a ground was a simple melody, and a descant an accompanying melody (sometimes improvised) played or sung above it

Play the maid's part: like a girl, say 'no' but mean 'yes' (proverbial)

leads: roof. Roofs of large buildings were covered with sheets or strips of lead. In this case, a flat piece of roof where people could walk

dance attendance: am kept waiting

engross: fatten

beads: prayers

aloft: on the upper stage (see p.12 above)

shouldered in: pushed aside into

successively: by right of inheritance

empery: legitimate authority

seasoned with: alleviated by, made more acceptable by

checked: would be rebuking

Unmeritable: unable to claim merit

royal fruit: Prince Edward

stealing: slow-moving, gently gliding

seat of majesty: throne

respects ... are nice: considerations are unimportant

was he contract: he was betrothed

put off: repulsed, rejected

poor petitioner: Queen Elizabeth. In *3 Henry VI*, Edward IV's first meeting with Elizabeth is when she comes to him with a petition about her inheritance

purchase: booty

pitch: summit, top (especially the height to which a bird of prey soars)

declension: sinking, lowering of himself

bigamy: if it were true that Edward had been betrothed to either Lady Lucy or Lady Bona, his marriage with Elizabeth would have been bigamous and therefore invalid

some alive: the Duchess of York (see III.5.84–93)

remorse: pity

egally: equally

all estates: people of all kinds

Your mere enforcement shall acquittance me: the mere fact that you compelled me will free me from responsibility

Act IV Scene 1

Queen Elizabeth, the Duchess of York, the Lady Anne, and Dorset arrive at the Tower to visit the two young princes. Brakenbury refuses to admit them: the Lord Protector has forbidden all visits. Stanley (Derby) arrives to summon Anne to Westminster, to be crowned as Richard's queen. The women lament at the news that Richard is now king. Elizabeth tells Dorset to escape immediately from England, and to live with Richmond.

NOTES AND GLOSSARY:

niece:	here, grand-daughter
in the hand:	by the hand
gratulate:	greet, salute
take thy office from thee:	take over your functions
leave it:	give up my office
lace:	the cord fastening her corset together. In Shakespeare's time, ladies used stiffeners in their corsets, to give their figures a fashionable shape. In moments of great emotion, it was necessary for them to release this constriction
Despiteful:	cruel, evil
Richmond:	after the Lancastrian defeat at Tewkesbury (1471), Richmond had been taken to Brittany by his uncle Jasper Tudor, to escape from the Yorkists
counted:	acknowledged, recognised
ill-dispersing:	spreading evil
cockatrice:	a fabulous serpent which was hatched from a cock's egg, and which could kill by a look
inclusive verge:	enclosing circle (the crown)
Anointed:	as part of the coronation ceremony, the king and queen had holy oil poured on their heads
feed my humour:	gratify my feelings
that dear saint:	Henry VI (see I.2)
grossly:	stupidly
teen:	suffering, grief

Act IV Scene 2

Richard is now king, and ascends his throne with pomp. He tells Buckingham that he wants the two young princes to be killed, and asks for his agreement. Buckingham asks for time to consider, and goes off. Richard decides that Buckingham can no longer be trusted as an ally. He asks a page if he knows anybody who could be bribed to commit murder;

the page suggests Tyrrel, and Richard sends the page to fetch him. Stanley brings the news that Dorset has fled overseas to Richmond. Richard tells Catesby to spread rumours that Queen Anne is sick, and likely to die. He thinks it necessary to marry his niece Elizabeth to strengthen his position. Tyrrel comes, and agrees to kill the two princes in the Tower. Buckingham returns, and claims the reward which Richard had promised for his help; Richard treats him with contempt, and goes off followed by his court. Buckingham remembers what had happened to Hastings, and decides to go at once to Wales, before he loses his head.

NOTES AND GLOSSARY:

play the touch:	act as a touchstone (stone used for testing the quality of gold)
the bastards:	the two princes in the Tower
iron-witted:	dull, stupid
unrespective:	inattentive, thoughtless
considerate:	thoughtful
witty:	sagacious, prudent, intelligent
The boy:	Clarence's son
it stands me much upon:	it matters very much to me
my brother's daughter:	Princess Elizabeth, daughter to Edward IV and sister to the princes in the Tower
Prove:	test, try
token:	Richard gives him something which will ensure his access to the princes—a signet-ring, perhaps
Jack:	(a) figure of a man which strikes the bell on the outside of a clock; (b) low fellow, scoundrel
keep'st the stroke:	keep on striking
Brecknock:	a manor in South Wales, belonging to Buckingham

Act IV Scene 3

In a soliloquy, Tyrrel describes how the two princes in the Tower have been murdered. He reports this to Richard. Ratcliffe brings the news that the Bishop of Ely has fled to join Richmond, and that Buckingham is in the field with an army of Welshmen. Richard makes preparations for war.

NOTES AND GLOSSARY:

fleshed:	experienced at killing, hardened
alablaster:	alabaster (a smooth white stone)
replenished:	complete, perfect
prime creation:	beginning of the world

Abraham's bosom: a phrase used in the Bible to mean 'heaven' (Luke 16:22)
Britain: Breton, inhabitant of Brittany (Bretagne) (see note to IV.1.42 above)
knot: marriage
Morton: John Morton, Bishop of Ely
fearful commenting: frightened discussion
expedition: speed, rapid action
Jove's Mercury: in Roman mythology, Jove (or Jupiter) was king of the gods, and Mercury his messenger or herald
brave: behave defiantly in

Act IV Scene 4

Queen Margaret comments while Queen Elizabeth and the Duchess of York lament the disasters that have befallen their families. Margaret triumphs over them: it is a member of their own family, Richard, who has preyed on them; and he too will shortly be destroyed. She leaves them, to return to France. Richard enters, leading his army; Queen Elizabeth and the Duchess reproach him for his crimes. The Duchess solemnly curses him, and leaves. Richard asks Queen Elizabeth to speak on his behalf to her daughter Elizabeth, whom he wishes to marry; after a long argument, she appears to agree. Ratcliffe brings Richard the news that a powerful navy is riding off the west coast, thought to be commanded by Richmond. Stanley confirms this news; Richard accuses him of disloyalty; Stanley protests his loyalty, and Richard allows him to go away to raise his forces, but makes him leave behind his son George as a hostage. A series of messengers brings news of rebellions against Richard, but one reports that Buckingham's army has been dispersed. Catesby reports that Buckingham has been captured, but that Richmond has landed at Milford. Richard orders his army to march towards Salisbury to encounter Richmond.

NOTES AND GLOSSARY:
induction: prologue, preface
sweets: fragrant flowers
quit: requite, balance out. She is referring to her own son, Edward, who was also murdered
Dead life ... tedious days: the Duchess is addressing herself
seniory: seniority
frown on the upper hand: have precedence in expressing themselves
holp'st: helped
had his teeth: it was said that Richard already had teeth when he was born (see also II.4.27–8)

galled:	made sore by rubbing
excellent:	outstandingly (with no implication of goodness)
pew-fellow:	companion
boot:	something additional included with a bargain to make up the value
intelligencer:	spy, secret agent
a-high:	on high, aloft. The reference is to the Wheel of Fortune
shot:	marksman
sign:	(a) flag, ensign; (b) mere effigy
fill the scene:	make up the numbers on the stage (like an actress with a walking-on part)
Decline:	recite in order
caitiff:	captive, wretch
wheeled:	rotated, turned
succeeders:	heirs
exclaims:	outcries
owed:	owned
the Lord's anointed:	a reference to the view that kings were God's deputies on earth
entreat me fair:	speak politely to me
I have stayed:	that is, when he was born
age confirmed:	settled age, maturity
comfortable:	bringing comfort, cheering
Humphrey Hour:	this reference has not been satisfactorily explained
level:	aim
opposite:	adverse, unfavourable. A reference to the common belief that character and destiny were determined by the position of the heavenly bodies at the time of one's birth
unavoided:	unavoidable
when avoided ... destiny:	when somebody who has banished grace (Richard) determines people's destinies
Whose hand ... lanched:	whoever's hand pierced
demise:	give, grant
So:	provided that
Lethe:	in Greek mythology, a river in the underworld; anyone who drank from Lethe immediately forgot the past
date:	duration, period of existence
humour:	temperament, disposition
conveyance with:	removal of
spoil:	destruction, harm, injury
quicken:	give life to

increase:	progeny, descendants
one pain:	that is, of childbirth
bid:	endured
Advantaging:	increasing the value of
retail:	tell the story of
Caesar:	the first Roman emperors took the name 'Caesar' as a title, so that it came to mean 'Roman emperor'
the King's king:	God. Marriage with a brother's daughter was forbidden
George ... Garter:	the Order of the Garter is the highest order of English knighthood. The George is a jewel bearing an image of St George which is worn by knights of this order
Hereafter time:	in the future
spicery:	spices. Referring to the Phoenix, a mythical bird, the only one of its kind, which lived in the Arabian desert. After five hundred years it burnt itself to ashes on a nest of sweet-smelling twigs, but then emerged from the ashes with renewed youth
recomforture:	consolation
hull:	float, drift
Hoyday:	an exclamation indicating surprise or mock-surprise
White-livered runagate:	cowardly vagabond
Welshman:	Richmond's father, Edmund Tudor, was Welsh
Devonshire ... Kent ... Yorkshire:	counties in the south-west, south-east, and north of England respectively. The impression is given that there are revolts against Richard all over the country
competitors:	associates
owls:	the cry of the owl was believed to forebode death
Dorsetshire:	a county in south-west England
Hoised:	hoisted
Milford:	Milford Haven, a port in South Wales

Act IV Scene 5

Stanley sends a messenger to Richmond explaining that his son George is held as a hostage, so that he dare not openly support Richmond yet. He also reports that Queen Elizabeth has agreed that Richmond shall marry her daughter Elizabeth.

NOTES AND GLOSSARY:

sty:	pig-house. The 'boar' is Richard

hold: custody, imprisonment
Pembroke ... Ha'rfordwest: Pembroke and Haverfordwest, towns in South Wales
bend their power: direct their forces

Act V Scene 1

Buckingham is being led to execution. He recognises the justice of God in punishing him for breaking his oath of loyalty to Edward IV and his family. He recalls the prophecy of Margaret, now fulfilled.

NOTES AND GLOSSARY:
All Souls' Day: 2 November, observed in the Church as a day of remembrance for the faithful Christian dead
my body's doomsday: the day of my body's death
in King Edward's time: see II.1.32–40. In that speech, however, Buckingham says nothing about All Souls' Day
determined respite ... wrongs: fixed time to which the punishment of my evil acts has been postponed
That high All-seer: God
Margaret's curse: see I.3.296–300

Act V Scene 2

Richmond and his supporters have marched across England without opposition. Richmond has received a letter of encouragement from Stanley. Richard's forces are now only one day's march away, and Richmond's army sets off cheerfully to encounter them.

NOTES AND GLOSSARY:
bowels: centre
wash: liquid kitchen-waste used for feeding pigs
embowelled: disembowelled, ripped open
Leicester: a large town in the east Midlands, about a hundred miles north of London
Tamworth: a town in the west Midlands, about twenty miles west of Leicester

---

Act V Scene 3

Evening, near Market Bosworth. The armies of Richard and of Richmond have come together, and a battle will be fought the following morning. Richard's tent is erected, and Richard and his followers go off to examine the lie of the land. Richmond's tent is erected, and Richmond sends a secret message to Stanley, whose forces are some distance from Richard's main army. Richard and his followers return; Richard sends a message to Stanley, ordering him to bring his forces to the battle by sunrise, otherwise his son will be killed. Richard goes into his tent and sleeps, and his followers go off. Stanley visits Richmond secretly, and promises to give all the help he can. Richmond is left alone in his tent; he prays to God for help in the battle, and then sleeps. The ghosts of those whom Richard had murdered come in turn and speak to Richard and to Richmond in their dreams: they speak encouragingly to Richmond, but threateningly to Richard. Richard awakes in terror, tortured by his conscience. Ratcliffe comes to tell him that it is nearly morning, and time to arm. Richmond's lords come to his tent to awaken him; he makes an oration to his army, and they go off to the battle. Richard gives instructions for the battle, and sends a message to Stanley ordering him to bring his forces. Richard makes an oration to his army. A messenger reports that Stanley refuses to come. Richmond's army is already advancing, and it is too late to execute George Stanley before the battle. Richard and his followers go off to the battle.

NOTES AND GLOSSARY:

Bosworth:	Market Bosworth, a small town about ten miles west of Leicester. The battle was fought a couple of miles south of the town
all's one for that:	it's all the same, it doesn't matter
descried:	discovered, spied out
battalia:	army in battle array
vantage:	features which will give a military advantage
sound direction:	solid ability as commanders
Richmond's tent:	Richard's tent and Richmond's are on the stage at the same time, presumably one on each side: see p.12 in Part 1 above
tract:	course, path
car:	chariot. In classical mythology, the sun was a fiery chariot drawn by horses and driven by the sun-god
form:	arrangement, formation
model:	plan, diagram
Limit ... to his several charge:	assign ... to his separate task
keeps:	remains with
beaver:	moveable face-guard on a helmet
Stir with the lark:	rise very early
pursuivant-at-arms:	a junior officer of the College of Heralds, of lower rank than a herald
watch:	watch-light, a candle marked into sections for measuring the passage of time

white Surrey:	the name of one of Richard's horses
staves:	spear-shafts
cockshut time:	twilight, dusk
Richard ... sleeps:	Richard remains visible to the audience, as we see when the ghosts address him (l.119)
our loving mother:	Richmond uses the royal plural, as if he were already king
flaky:	resembling snowflakes (because of the coming light, which makes clouds visible)
mortal-staring:	killing with its look (like a basilisk)
leisure:	short time available
peise:	weigh
bruising irons:	iron weapons which crush with heavy blows
Enter the Ghost:	the ghosts enter in the order of their deaths, beginning with Prince Edward of Lancaster (killed at Tewkesbury in 1471) and ending with Buckingham (executed in 1483, two years before the Battle of Bosworth). The procession thus summarises Richard's bloody career
fulsome:	excessive, cloying
lights burn blue:	this was believed to indicate the presence of a ghost
Cold ... drops:	of sweat
proof:	impenetrable armour
Cry mercy:	I ask your pardon
leisure and enforcement:	shortness and compulsion
fat:	plenty, choicest produce
quits:	(will) repay. A plural: see p.22 in Part 1 above
Tell:	count
by the book:	according to the calendar (almanac)
braved:	made splendid
will not be seen:	refuses to shine
foreward:	vanguard
main battle:	central body of the army
winged:	flanked
Saint George to boot:	with St George (the patron saint of England) helping us
direction:	battle-order
Jockey:	a familiar form of John, Norfolk's name
Dickon:	a familiar form of Richard, like 'Dickie'
join:	join battle
sort:	band, company
lackey:	servile. A lackey was a camp-follower
distrain:	seize, confiscate
distain:	defile, dishonour

stragglers:	vagabonds, tramps. Vagabondage was illegal; the vagabond was punished by being whipped and sent back to his own parish
Amaze:	stupefy, terrify
welkin:	sky
staves:	lances, spears
spleen:	courage, spirit

Act V Scene 4

The battle. Richard is performing incredible feats of arms. His horse has been killed, and he is seeking Richmond on foot. But, despite his feats, the position of his army is critical.

NOTES AND GLOSSARY:

opposite:	opponent, adversary
set ... cast:	staked my life on one throw of the dice
stand ... die:	accept the danger of the dice
six Richmonds:	presumably a number of people in Richmond's army had been dressed like him, to cause confusion

Act V Scene 5

Richard and Richmond meet and fight; Richard is killed. Stanley presents Richmond with the crown, taken from Richard's head. He reports that George Stanley is alive and safe. In a final speech to his followers, Richmond proclaims a pardon to Richard's soldiers if they submit to him. He promises to fulfil his undertaking to marry Princess Elizabeth of York, thus uniting the warring houses of York and Lancaster. He looks back on the madness of the civil wars, and prays that henceforth England may enjoy peace and prosperity.

NOTES AND GLOSSARY:

Retreat:	signal to retire (sounded on drums and trumpets)
flourish:	a fanfare on brass instruments, especially used to signify the approach of a person of high rank
royalty:	the crown
ta'en the sacrament:	sworn to do
White Rose ... Red:	the white rose was the emblem of the house of York, the red rose that of the house of Lancaster
conjunction:	union, marriage
amen:	an expression of agreement with a prayer or a wish
Abate the edge:	make blunt the swords
reduce:	bring back

Part 3

Commentary

Date and sources

The first known reference to *Richard III* occurs in 1597, but the play was probably written a few years earlier: its style and dramatic techniques suggest that it was one of Shakespeare's earliest plays, probably composed about 1593.

The main sources for the play are two sixteenth-century history books: Edward Hall's *Union of the Two Noble and Illustrate Families of Lancaster and York* (1548) and Raphael Holinshed's *Chronicles of England, Scotland, and Ireland* (1577), of which Shakespeare used the enlarged edition of 1587. Both Hall and Holinshed drew heavily on Sir Thomas More's Latin *Historia Ricardi Tertii (History of King Richard III)*, written 1513–14, and on Polydore Vergil's *Historia Anglica* (1534). Shakespeare probably drew on other sources as well—historical works, poems, plays. Hall and Holinshed, however, were the principal sources.

Shakespeare shaped this historical material to make it into a play. *Richard III* has a complex structure, with a number of clear themes, and to produce such a play Shakespeare had to select, compress, change the chronological order of events, and even invent new incidents. The early part of the play depicts the funeral of Henry VI, Richard's marriage to Anne, the murder of Clarence, and the death of Edward IV; these are all made to seem closely connected in time, with Richard stage-managing events. But in fact Henry VI died in 1471 and Richard married Anne in 1472, while Clarence was not sent to the Tower until 1477 and was executed in 1478; and the death of Edward IV was even later, not taking place until 1483. Events are similarly compressed in the later part of the play: Shakespeare makes it seem as though Buckingham's rebellion took place shortly before the Battle of Bosworth, whereas two years elapsed between the two events; and the various risings which are reported to Richard in IV.4.498–519 in fact took place at different dates. Many historical incidents are omitted: there is no mention of Richmond's unsuccessful attempt to invade England in 1483, or of the fact that Richard and Anne had a son (who died in 1484).

Shakespeare altered history to suit his purposes, and invented whole episodes. The presence of Queen Margaret in the play is unhistorical: she was captured at Tewkesbury in 1471, and held prisoner by Edward IV for four years; she was then sent back to France, where she died in 1482 (a year before Edward IV). Shakespeare, however, makes her into a major figure in the play. Shakespeare makes Richard responsible for the murder of Clarence, but in fact Clarence was given a public trial and was executed. The episode where Richard woos Anne is Shakespeare's own invention, and so is the imprisonment of Hastings. The character of Hastings is also Shakespeare's invention, as is that of Richmond: the historical Richmond was niggardly, cunning, and timorous, nothing like the noble and pious figure in the play. But the greatest invention of all is the character of Richard himself. Shakespeare's sources were written from the official Tudor point of view, and in them Richard was already depicted as a cruel, evil, hunchbacked tyrant; but on this basis Shakespeare developed the brilliant stage personality that dominates the play.

As a result of this shaping of the source material, a clear interpretation of English history emerges. Usurpation, which is a breach of the divinely decreed order of the universe, leads to civil war and chaos; wrong provokes counter-wrong, murder follows murder; but God's justice ultimately strikes down all those that commit evil; Richard himself is one of God's instruments of punishment, as well as being the last to be punished; and, through God's providence, chaos and war finally give way to peace and order, when Richmond, God's champion, overthrows the incarnation of evil and establishes the Tudor monarchy, uniting the warring houses of York and Lancaster, and inaugurating an age of peace and prosperity.

Senecan and popular influences

In early Shakespeare plays, we see the successful fusion of various dramatic traditions—popular, academic, courtly. *Richard III* shows the strong influence of Roman drama, especially of the first-century writer Seneca, and it is perhaps the most Senecan of his plays. Seneca's plays always have a Chorus, and this is absent from Shakespeare's play; but the joint lamentations by characters such as Queen Elizabeth and the Duchess of York give a choric effect (for instance, II.2.62–88; IV.1.87–96; IV.4.9–60). The use of ghosts and of the supernatural is common in Seneca; and in *Richard III* there is a whole procession of ghosts (V.3.119–77), an extensive use of omens and prophecies, and a vivid description of the underworld (I.4.43–63), a favourite Senecan theme. Seneca's plays are imbued with a spirit of violence, bloodshed, and physical horrors; *Richard III* has nothing resembling the most repulsive horrors of Seneca, but it too is full of violence, with such episodes as the murder of Clarence and of the two young princes, the execution of Hastings and the bringing of his head to Richard, the executions of Rivers, Grey, Vaughan, and Buckingham, and the frequent descriptions of bloody deeds committed in the past. Seneca tends to use certain stock characters, and one of these, the cruel tyrant, perhaps contributes to the character of Richard (which however contains many other elements). Seneca frequently refers to the Furies (avenging goddesses who come from Hades to punish and torment men), and even introduces a Fury as a character in the prologue to one of his plays; and in *Richard III* Queen Margaret resembles an avenging Fury, urging on men and the heavens to blood and revenge. Despite the violence, Seneca's plays are full of reflection and self-examination: characters analyse themselves in soliloquy. Richard, too, makes great use of soliloquy, explaining himself and his motives to the audience, and in one soliloquy (V.3.180–207) he is driven to self-examination. In style, Seneca often uses an elaborate rhetoric, with exaggerations and lengthy descriptions; and *Richard III*, too, cultivates elaborate rhetorical devices. But at times Seneca uses stichomythia, cut-and-thrust dialogue in which two characters throw single lines at each other in turn. Shakespeare imitates this, for example in the interchange between Richard and Queen Elizabeth beginning 'Infer fair England's peace by this alliance' (IV.4.343). At other times, Seneca indulges in passages of conventional moralising; he is particularly fond of proverbs, and of epigrams (brief, pointed, polished statements). Richard, too, is fond of proverbs, and of epigrammatic moralising, such as:

> They that stand high have many blasts to shake them,
> And if they fall, they dash themselves to pieces.
>
> (I.3.258–59)

There are also episodes in *Richard III* which remind one of episodes in Seneca: Richard's wooing of Anne (I.2) bears some resemblance to an episode in Seneca's *Hercules Furens*.

But, while *Richard III* shows strong Senecan influence, it is also very different from Seneca; and one reason for this, clearly, is that it was written for the English public theatre (not, like Seneca's plays, for recitation to a coterie audience), and is deeply influenced by the popular English dramatic tradition. There is more action than in Seneca, more interplay between characters, more twists and turns in the dramatic situation, and less moralising and reflection. The influence of the medieval moral play is seen in the conflict of good and evil in *Richard III*, and in their ritual opposition, as in the dream episode in V.3. Richard, who is frequently referred to as a devil or an agent of Hell, is a type of evil, in conflict with the representatives of good, and indeed with God himself. But in the medieval religious plays, devils and representatives of evil sometimes developed into comic characters, and Richard actually compares himself to one such stock character of the moral plays, the Vice or Iniquity (III.1.82). This element in Richard comes out in his humour and his clowning, for example in the episode where he and Buckingham dress up in rotten old armour and pretend to be terrified, for the benefit of the Lord Mayor (III.5.1–20). This linking of the comic with evil characters is also seen in the two murderers of Clarence (I.4.101–60).

The structure of the play

Medieval influence is perhaps also seen in the large-scale structure of the play, which depicts the rise of the central character, followed by his decline. This reminds us of the medieval and renaissance idea of the Wheel of Fortune, on which men were lifted up and then carried down. The rise-fall pattern is later used by Shakespeare in many of his tragedies: the central character increases in power or prosperity until about the middle of the play, but then declines and eventually meets his death. This pattern is clearly seen in *Richard III*. In the first part of the play, Richard removes the obstacles between himself and the throne— Clarence, the Queen's relatives, Hastings. The way is now clear for the charade in which he is offered the crown, and in IV.2 we see him as king, at the peak of his power. At once, however, there is a sharp reverse in his fortunes: in the very same scene in which he appears as king, his alliance with Buckingham ends, and we hear that Dorset has fled abroad to join Richmond. Other reverses follow: the Bishop of Ely flees to Richmond, revolts against Richard are reported in many parts of the country, and Richmond lands in Wales and raises an army. Queen Elizabeth and Stanley correspond secretly with Richmond, and, in the final decisive battle at Bosworth, Stanley's defection plays a part in Richard's defeat and death.

The play thus falls clearly into two parts: in Acts I to III we see Richard's rise to power, and in Acts IV and V his decline and fall. Within both parts, however, he undergoes fluctuations of fortune. In the earlier part of the play he has his setbacks, like the failure of Buckingham to win the support of the London citizens (III.7.1–40). In the later part of the play, conversely, he has his successes, as when Buckingham's army is dispersed and Buckingham captured (IV.4.510–13, 531). These fluctuations of fortune help to maintain the suspense, but they take place within the broader pattern of Richard's rise and fall.

Within this main plot are included numerous episodes involving other characters, all related to the central story. The main ones are concerned with the death of Clarence, the winning of Anne and her later regrets, the blindness and fall of Hastings, the outmanoeuvring of the Queen's party, the coming to London of Prince Edward, Buckingham's alliance with Richard and their later quarrel, and the gradual emergence of Stanley as an important opponent of Richard.

But there is another kind of structure in *Richard III*. It is a highly patterned play, which makes great use of parallel episodes. Often, a scene or episode in the early part of the play has a counterpart in the later part of the play, but with some significant difference. In I.2, Richard woos the Lady Anne; in IV.4 he woos the Princess Elizabeth, through her mother. In both cases the proposed match is, on the face of it, preposterous. But whereas the first wooing is successful, the second is not, for we learn later that the Queen has agreed to a marriage between Elizabeth and Richmond. In I.4, Clarence recounts a dream, in which he goes to Hell and is denounced for perjury and murder; in V.3, Richard has a dream, in which he is denounced by the souls of those whom he had murdered. Clarence expresses penitence for his crimes, and prays to God for mercy; but when Richard wakes he expresses no contrition and utters no prayer, even though he is terrified by his dream. Similarly, there are parallel scenes of cursing (I.3.187–232 and IV.4.136–98), and parallel scenes of lamentation (II.2.34–88 and IV.4.9–46); and here too there are significant differences between the earlier episodes and the later ones.

Often, too, there is a pattern within a single scene. The opening scene of the play has the following structure: (1) soliloquy by Richard; (2) conversation with Clarence; (3) soliloquy by Richard; (4) conversation with Hastings; (5) soliloquy by Richard. Moreover, there are parallels between (2) and (4): Richard is deceiving both Clarence and Hastings, and explains his deceit in the following soliloquies; and Clarence is being taken to the Tower, while Hastings is coming from it. This patterning in the opening scene suggests that there is nothing accidental or casual about the events depicted: they are manipulated by Richard, but also, on a larger scale, they show the working of God's providence.

In V.3 there is a somewhat different kind of pattern within the scene, which gives a strongly ritual quality to the drama. Richard's tent is pitched on one side of the stage, Richmond's on the other, and each leader in turn consults his chief followers and makes his plans for the following day. Both of them send a message to Stanley. When they sleep, the ghosts of Richard's victims appear in turn and speak to them in their dreams, first to Richard and then to Richmond. Many similar phrases are used by the various ghosts: to Richard, *Let me sit heavy on thy soul tomorrow*, and *despair and die*; to Richmond, *comfort, live and flourish, awake*. The whole effect of this dream sequence, therefore, is highly formal and ritualistic. Finally, after awaking from their dreams, both Richard and Richmond make an oration to their army. The patterns produce a symbolic effect, suggesting a confrontation of good with evil.

The structural patterns in the play help to evoke a sense of the world order that Richard is attacking. The events of the play may seem chaotic and anarchic, but the universe itself is not: there is a social order and a moral order, and in the end these triumph.

Characterisation

Richard the Machiavellian villain

Richard is completely self-centred, caring for nobody but himself. He aims at personal power, and in pursuing it he has no moral scruples; he is ruthless and vindictive; he has no belief in religion; he is cruel, hypocritical, and blasphemous. He is in fact a variant on a theatrical type of the time, the Machiavellian villain. The great Italian political thinker Niccolò Machiavelli (1469–1527) had argued in his book *The Prince* (written in 1513) that politics must be separated from ethics: the ruler of a state must disregard questions of morality, and be guided only by the end which he is aiming at. Reasons of state, or policy, are more important than conscience. The self-centred immoral villain of late Elizabethan drama is a travesty of these ideas: few people in England at that time had read Machiavelli, and their ideas about him were derived at second hand.

The individualism and self-centredness of the Machiavellian villain can be compared to the attitudes of the New Men in Elizabethan England—the capitalist landlords and entrepreneurs whose economic individualism brought them into conflict with customary attitudes and behaviour, which were communal. Professor Siegel* has compared the attitudes of Richard III to those of the Elizabethan businessman. He calls particular attention to Richard's language: he often uses trading terms, like 'a packhorse in his great affairs' (I.3.121), and also financial and monetary terms, like 'advantaging their loan with interest' (IV.3.323). Moreover, he is twice referred to as a *factor*, that is a business agent (III.7.133; IV.4.72). Richard's brutal energy, Siegel argues, is the energy of the bourgeoisie.

But at the same time, as Siegel also remarks, Richard is of high birth, coming from an ancient noble family, and he is very proud of his birth. He constantly sneers at the parvenus, the relatives of the Queen who have been made into great noblemen almost overnight. Partly this is a political ploy, to stir up discord between the Queen's party and the rest of the nobility. But his pride in his rank seems genuine, as when he says to Dorset, one of the new noblemen:

> but I was born so high.
> Our aery buildeth in the cedar's top
> And dallies with the wind and scorns the sun.
>
> (I.3.262–4)

---

*Paul N. Siegel, 'Richard III as Businessman', in *Shakespeare Jahrbuch*, Band 114, Weimar, 1978.

Richard, in fact, wants to have it both ways: he attacks the established order, but also wants to be head of it.

Richard, then, has characteristics both of the bourgeois individualist and of the turbulent feudal nobleman. This combination of apparently discordant characteristics is found in other characters in the drama of the time, and is not really surprising. The Elizabethan political order was threatened from both sides: on the one hand there was the old-fashioned feudal nobility, who had rebelled against Elizabeth in 1569; on the other hand there were the New Men, the capitalist landlords, the Puritans. It is understandable that these different threats to the Elizabethan order should be conflated in a figure such as Richard III.

Richard's moral choice

Richard's Machiavellian outlook is represented as a deliberate moral choice. In the opening speech of the play he says:

I am determined to prove a villain

(I.1.30)

He dislikes the pleasures of peace, and wants war or dangerous and exciting activity. It is true that, as one of his motives for this choice, he mentions his physical deformity, which makes him unsuited to love (I.1.14–29). But he is not presented as a victim of this deformity, finding some kind of psychological compensation in destructive activity. Rather, we see his physical deformity as an outward expression of his inner, moral deformity; and his moral choice is made with cool intelligence, not in anguish. An even clearer statement of Richard's moral choice is to be found near the end of *3 Henry VI*. There, after the Battle of Tewkesbury, Richard hurries to London and murders Henry VI, saying:

Down, down to hell, and say I sent thee thither,
I that have neither pity, love, nor fear.
(*3 Henry VI*, V.6.67–8)

He then considers his physical deformity, and expresses his philosophy:

I have no brother, I am like no brother;
And this word love, which greybeards call divine,
Be resident in men like one another,
And not in me. I am myself alone.
(*3 Henry VI*, V.6.78–83)

That is his choice: the rejection of love and brotherhood, the embracing of egotism and self-sufficiency—'I am myself alone'. At the end of *Richard III*, Richard comes to see the consequences for himself of this moral choice. The night before Bosworth Field, he awakes in terror from his nightmare, tormented by his conscience. When his conscience has accused him, he says:

> I shall despair. There is no creature loves me;
> And if I die, no soul will pity me.
>
> (V.3.201–2)

But that is exactly what he had chosen: he had rejected love and pity, and chosen to be himself alone. This theme, the discovery of the implications of one's moral choices, is to be richly developed in Shakespeare's subsequent plays. Here, it is somewhat crudely handled, since there is no gradual realisation by Richard, but simply one tormented moment caused by his dream. But it gives great moral force to the play.

What makes Richard attractive?

Although Richard is a cold-blooded villain, he is nevertheless a fascinating character, and it is he that holds the audience throughout the play. What gives him this attractiveness? First, he has great courage. His hypocrisy and his scheming are not the result of fear, for he is quite dauntless. This is seen when he confronts the halberdiers at the funeral of Henry VI, and terrifies them (I.2.33–42). With this courage goes his great prowess as a soldier, described by Catesby during the Battle of Bosworth:

> The King enacts more wonders than a man,
> Daring an opposite to every danger.
> His horse is slain, and all on foot he fights,
> Seeking for Richmond in the throat of death.
>
> (V.4.2–5)

This passage also suggests Richard's enormous energy: he is always busy, always planning, always bustling. When he acts, he does so with speed and decisiveness: this is seen when he decides to dispose of his wife Anne and to marry off Clarence's daughter to a nonentity (IV.2.49–54; IV.3.36–9), and when he dismisses Buckingham and arranges by himself for the murder of the princes in the Tower (IV.2.28–81). The energy is also an *intellectual* energy: we feel that Richard is more intelligent than his opponents, that his triumphs over them are triumphs of the mind. In his soliloquies, when he is planning his future moves, we have the sense of a mind buzzing with excitement:

> He cannot live, I hope, and must not die
> Till George be packed with post-horse up to heaven.
> I'll in, to urge his hatred more to Clarence

With lies well steeled with weighty arguments;
And, if I fail not in my deep intent,
Clarence hath not another day to live;
Which done, God take King Edward to his mercy
And leave the world for me to bustle in.

(I.1.145–52)

That passage illustrates two other qualities: Richard's humour, and his lively use of language, both seen in 'Till George be packed with post-horse up to heaven'. The humour is often grim:

Simple plain Clarence, I do love thee so
That I will shortly send thy soul to heaven,
If heaven will take the present at our hands.

(I.1.118–20)

There the humour lies in the sardonic last line, with its implication that Clarence will perhaps be destined for Hell rather than Heaven. The humour often finds expression in puns, as when Richard puns on *naught* (I.1.97–101), on *noble* (I.3.80–1), on *Jack* (IV.2.113). Sometimes the humour is at the expense of the innocent he is addressing, but relished only by himself and the audience, as when he says to Clarence:

O, belike his majesty hath some intent
That you should be new-christened in the Tower.

(I.1.49–50)

There Clarence sees part of the joke, which seems to be ridiculing the King for imprisoning a man on account of his name; but the audience knows what Richard is planning for Clarence in the Tower, and so sees also the joke at Clarence's expense. The humour is sometimes reinforced by rhyme, as in his mockery of Hastings:

And bid my lord, for joy of this good news,
Give Mistress Shore one gentle kiss the more.

(III.1.184–5)

The wit and the humour contribute to the liveliness of Richard's language. In addition, his speech is often marked by the use of vivid, concrete details, as when he describes himself as having been a *packhorse* (I.3.121), or compares upstarts and true noblemen to *wrens* and *eagles* (I.3.70), or says that Clarence is *franked up to fatting* (I.3.313), or remarks that the eyes of the murderers *drop millstones* instead of tears (I.3.352). This last example is a proverb, and Richard is fond of proverbial expressions, which tend to be concrete and homely; another example is 'But yet I run before my horse to market' (I.1.160).

Richard as actor

But what above all makes Richard a fascinating character is his skill as an actor. Like Falstaff and Hamlet, he is constantly playing a part, and enjoying it. In the first scene of the play, he acts the part of the devoted brother to Clarence; in the second scene, he acts the part of the devoted lover to Anne. To the court, he acts the part of the innocent man who is unjustly accused (I.3.42–61), of the plain man who cannot flatter (I.3.47–53), of the pious man who is too kind-hearted to get on in the world (I.3.139–41, 305–7; II.1.47–74). When he drops the bombshell about Clarence's death, he pretends to be affronted, but the whole thing is obviously calculated (II.1.79–81); and at the end of the scene (II.1.136–41) he stirs up trouble by pretending to believe that the Queen's party is responsible. He acts to his ally Buckingham, pretending that Buckingham is the brains of the partnership (II.2.151–4).In the council scene in the Tower, Richard comes in all affability and smiles (III.4.22–33), but at his second entry he is in a fury (III.4.59–79); it is clear that neither mood is his real one, and that they are simply pieces of acting to enable him to attain his ends. After the execution of Hastings, Richard and Buckingham amuse themselves with a bit of play-acting for the benefit of the Lord Mayor, pretending to be in terror of their lives (III.5.1–20); and Richard makes a pathetic speech about his affection for Hastings, and how he had been deceived in him (III.5.24–32). The play-acting reaches its climax in the scene at Baynard's Castle, when Buckingham offers the crown to Richard and Richard pretends to refuse; Richard appears on the leads with a prayer-book in his hand and a bishop on each side of him, and plays the part of the simple, pious, tender-hearted prince who is more concerned with religious meditation than with politics; and the zest with which he throws himself into his parts is well illustrated by the line in which he gently reproaches Buckingham for using bad language:

> BUCKINGHAM: Come citizens. Zounds! I'll entreat no more.
> RICHARD: O do not swear, my lord of Buckingham.
> (III.7.218–19)

After he has become king, Richard has less scope for acting: the attainment of the crown has been the object of all his scheming and acting; and once has has achieved it, he simply has to play the part of the king, and has less need to put on a turn.

Richard's acting is usually effective: he deceives most people (though not all) into believing that he is what he acts. His own brother Clarence is completely taken in by him (I.4.231–49), and so is Rivers (I.3.315–16), and so is Hastings, even to the extent of saying of Richard:

> I think there's never a man in Christendom
> Can lesser hide his love or hate than he,
> For by his face you straight shall know his heart.
>
> (III.4.51–3)

Hastings goes on to observe that Richard is not offended with anybody present. No sooner are the words out of his mouth than Richard enters in the simulated rage which sweeps Hastings to execution.

Do Richard's powers decline?

It is often said that, from the time he becomes king, Richard's powers decline, and he ceases to be the brilliant operator and manipulator that he was in the first half of the play.

At first, Richard is the initiator and contriver of almost everything that happens: he pulls the strings and controls the action. In the second half of the play, by contrast, many of his actions are responses to initiatives from his enemies. There are exceptions: he disposes of his wife Anne and of the children of Clarence, he arranges for the murder of the young princes, he tries to arrange a marriage with Princess Elizabeth. But increasingly his moves are reactions to those of his opponents—the rebellion of Buckingham, the invasion of Richmond. Formerly, Richard was the secret schemer against those in power; but now it is others that scheme against Richard: Stanley and Queen Elizabeth correspond with Richmond, and Stanley even has a secret meeting with him.

Moreover, Richard is no longer so overwhelmingly dominant, verbally and intellectually, as in the early part of the play. This is seen if one compares the wooing of Anne (I.2.49–224) with the wooing of Elizabeth (IV.4.199–430). In the earlier scene, Richard is brilliantly successful. In the later, he is out-talked by Queen Elizabeth, who has a stinging reply to every argument that he advances. The audience feels, moreover, that Richard is repeating himself, trying to perform the same trick twice. He even uses, though unsuccessfully, one of the arguments he had used to win Anne:

> Say that I did all this for love of her
>
> (IV.4.288)

Moreover, Queen Elizabeth outwits him: she appears to agree to his request, but we learn later (IV.5.7–8) that she has deceived him, and has agreed to the marriage with Richmond. Stanley, too, outwits Richard: by pretending loyalty, and deferring his volte-face until the very moment that the Battle of Bosworth begins (V.3.343–4), he manages to save his son's life and yet help Richmond. Richard, then, can be both out-talked and outwitted; and it is significant that, when he is confronted and accused by his mother and Queen Elizabeth (IV.4.136–48), he is reduced to drowning their voices by ordering drums and trumpets to sound.

Richard's character also deteriorates. In the early part of the play his moods, whether of affability or anger, are all part of his play-acting. But in the later part he is often genuinely tetchy and irritable, and with the irritability goes an unwonted inefficiency. This is seen in one episode with Catesby and Ratcliffe, when the latter has brought news about Richmond's invading navy:

RICHARD: Some light-foot friend post to the Duke of Norfolk:
Ratcliffe, thyself—or Catesby—where is he?
CATESBY: Here my good lord.
RICHARD: Catesby, fly to the Duke.
CATESBY: I will, my lord, with all convenient haste.
RICHARD: Ratcliffe, come hither. Post to Salisbury.
When thou com'st thither—Dull unmindful villain,
Why stay'st thou here and go'st not to the Duke?
CATESBY: First, mighty liege, tell me your highness pleasure,
What from your grace I shall deliver to him.
RICHARD: O true good Catesby; bid him levy straight
The greatest strength and power that he can make
And meet me suddenly at Salisbury.
CATESBY: I go. *Exit*
RATCLIFFE: What, may it please you, shall I do at Salisbury?
RICHARD: Why, what wouldst thou do there before I go?
RATCLIFFE: Your highness told me I should post before.
RICHARD: My mind is changed.

(IV.4.440–56)

Richard forgets to instruct Catesby, and then flies into a rage with him for not carrying out the instructions; he then forgets the orders he was about to give to Ratcliffe. A similar outburst of rage is seen later, when Richard strikes a messenger (IV.4.507–8). All this is in strong contrast to the self-control and calculated display of moods which he had shown earlier.

Moreover, whereas in the early part of the play Richard is supremely confident, in the later part he sometimes shows self-doubt and fear. In the very first scene in which he appears as king, we see the fear and uncertainty which now drive him on to further atrocities:

I must be married to my brother's daughter,
Or else my kingdom stands on brittle glass.
Murder her brothers, and then marry her—
Uncertain way of gain! But I am in
So far in blood that sin will pluck on sin.

(IV.2.59–63)

It is not until Act IV that we hear from Anne how Richard keeps her awake at night with his 'timorous dreams' (IV.1.84); this clearly refers to Richard as he was earlier in the play, but the audience does not hear about it until late in the play, so that it affects their view of his character at that stage, not earlier. This speech of Anne's prepares us for Richard's terrified awakening from his dream the night before Bosworth (V.3.178–207); there, he is tormented by his conscience, and we see that he is not the completely self-sufficient character which he had imagined himself. He is so shaken by the dream that he even admits his fear to Ratcliffe, and asks him for reassurance (V.3.213–16).

There are many other small touches in the later part of the play which help to suggest Richard's moodiness, irritability and self-doubt: before Bosworth, he wonders where he will lie the following night (V.3.8), and admits that he lacks his usual 'alacrity of spirit' and 'cheer of mind' (V.3.73–4). Nevertheless, he remains a formidable character to the end, with enormous energy and fighting spirit: he leads his army into battle in a mood of exaltation and ferocious determination (V.3.339–42, 348–52), and in our last view of him in the play (V.4) he is fighting on foot in the front line of battle, enacting more wonders than a man, and 'Seeking for Richmond in the throat of death'.

The attractive wicked character

Richard, then, has many attractive qualities—courage, military prowess, energy, intelligence, humour, a vivid use of language, a love of play-acting, and an enormous zest; and he continues to have many of these qualities right to the end, even if he does undergo some decline. But at the same time Richard is a monster of wickedness, as is made abundantly clear. He is therefore a classic example of the attractive wicked character, a type not uncommon in literature. Such characters often raise problems of interpretation for the reader: in theory it may be possible to distinguish between a character's attractive qualities and his wickedness, but in practice the two are often difficult to separate, and we may therefore feel that we are being invited to admire wickedness. In the case of Richard, there can be no doubt that we are expected to condemn his cold-blooded and self-centred evil. But does his attractiveness nevertheless undermine some of the things which the play seems to be saying? In particular, does it undermine the Tudor Myth, the view of history which the play seems to present—the Tudors as the bringers of peace and prosperity and legitimacy, the combiners of the white rose and the red? Some critics have taken the view that it does. A.P. Rossiter,* for example, argues that, while Shakespeare in *Richard III* is by no means

* A.P. Rossiter, 'Angel with Horns: the Unity of *Richard III*', in *Shakespeare: the Histories*, ed. E.M. Waith, Prentice-Hall, Englewood Cliffs, New Jersey, 1965, pp.66–84.

debunking or disproving the Tudor Myth, he is not entirely endorsing it, but is leaving us, not with absolutes or certainties, but with 'relatives, ambiguities, irony, a process thoroughly dialectical'.

The other characters in the play

Richard dominates the play, and his character is the only one which is developed at length: the remaining characters are relatively slight sketches. The only one who can compete with Richard in energy and force of character is Queen Margaret, and she is not really involved in the action of the play, but is a commentator and prophetess. She resembles Richard not only in her energy but in the wickedness of her deeds: in the scene where she confronts the court, Richard reminds her of the murder of the child Rutland, and of the way she had taunted his father about it; she too was cursed for her cruelty, and suffered retribution (I.3.173–80). But she also differs greatly from Richard: where he is cool and calculating and ironic, she is fiercely passionate, denouncing and cursing her enemies with hatred and anger, and gloating triumphantly over their disasters (see IV.4.1–125).

Hastings is a study in over-confidence and blindness. He is loyal to Edward IV and his sons, but lacks the understanding of people and the political skill to make that loyalty effective. He takes part in the factional rivalries of the court, rejoices at the execution of Rivers, Vaughan, and Grey (III.2.51–2), and even hopes to send more enemies the same way (III.2.60–1); but he fails to take warning from their fate, or from the advice of Stanley (III.2.10–18, 74–88). He completely misinterprets the character of Richard (III.4.48–57), and is quite blind to his impending doom. His blindness is made all the more striking by the bluntness of Catesby's approach to him about Richard's designs on the crown (III.2.38–50). Buckingham has instructed Catesby to sound out Hastings 'as it were afar off' (III.1.170), to see if he would support Richard; but in fact Catesby shows no subtlety at all in his approach, but quite baldly states Richard's aims and his hope for Hastings's support (III.2.46–7). Despite this clear intimation of what is afoot, Hastings is still quite blind to his danger.

Clarence is another who is deceived by Richard: he is unable to credit the statement by the murderers that it is Richard who has hired them to kill him (I.4.231–50). Clarence genuinely repents the crimes of murder and perjury that he has committed, and prays to God that at least his innocent wife and children may escape punishment (I.4.69–72). In his argument with the murderers he eloquently presents religious views and wins one of the murderers over, though this is not enough to save him.

Buckingham is by no means an innocent: he is politic, prudent, the 'deep-revolving witty Buckingham' (IV.2.42); yet in the end he too is deceived and discarded by Richard. Buckingham disregards the warning of Margaret (I.3.288–95), and allies himself with Richard; but it requires only one hesitation by Buckingham (about the proposed murder of the princes), and Richard discards him with contempt (IV.2). Buckingham, unlike Hastings, reads the signs immediately, but he too ends as Richard's victim.

Many of Richard's victims are themselves guilty of murder or perjury, and their fate can be seen as divine retribution; this is true of Clarence, Rivers, Grey, Hastings, and Buckingham. Some of Richard's victims, however, are innocent. This is true of the two young princes: their family may be guilty of political crimes, for which they suffer, but they are not personally guilty. Prince Edward, in the single scene where he appears (III.1), is dignified and princely, accepting his position without affectation. He makes clear his views on the arrest of his mother's relatives, but knows his own powerlessness. His meditations on the Tower and Julius Caesar are thoughtful and mature, and lead on to his kingly ambition to 'win our ancient right in France again' (III.1.92), which to the Elizabethan audience would have seemed a proper and laudable desire. Prince Richard, by contrast, is precocious and witty, mocking other people and himself; and his taunts are sufficiently pointed to rile his uncle (III.1.154–6). The mother of these two princes, Queen Elizabeth, is another innocent victim. In a difficult position at court, she behaves with dignity and restraint in the face of the sneers of Richard (I.3.62–109). After the death of Edward IV she is powerless, and can do little but lament. Indeed, lamentation, often choric, is a mark of the innocent helpless characters in the play—Elizabeth, Anne, the Duchess of York, the children of Clarence.

The good character who is not helpless, Richmond, is a slightly-drawn and pallid character compared to Richard; he is simply the virtuous, religious, and heroic figure devoted to his country's good, an instrument of God. The other good character who, in the second half of the play, emerges as a positive force opposing Richard is Lord Stanley (also called Derby, though in historical fact he did not become Earl of Derby until after the Battle of Bosworth). He sees the danger from Richard, but is unable to persuade Hastings of it (III.2.1–34, 72–93). When Hastings is executed, he saves himself (like the rest of the council) by keeping his mouth shut and in effect acquiescing. Richard suspects him, because Richmond is his step-son, and he has to behave with great care and circumspection; but by protestations of loyalty to Richard and a careful timing of his defection to Richmond he is able to contribute to the latter's victory and yet save the life of his son, held hostage by Richard. In Stanley's hypocritical protestations of loyalty, and his secret intrigues against Richard, we see Richard's own weapons turned against him, and used by the forces of good.

Style and language

The past and the future

The play frequently reminds the audience of events in the past, especially the civil wars, with their deeds of cold-blooded murder and the breaking of faith. Margaret, calling for revenge for the wrongs she has suffered, refers to the past particularly often; but the horrors of the civil wars are referred to frequently by many other characters too. One of the episodes most often called to mind is the murder of Prince Edward of Lancaster at Tewkesbury (see I.2.91–7, 239–49; I.3.119, 191ff.; I.4.52–6, 209–25; III.3.16; V.3.119–21). Other episodes frequently recalled are the murder of Henry VI, the killing of Rutland and of the Duke of York after the Battle of Wakefield, and the defection of Clarence to the Lancastrians and his subsequent return to the Yorkist side. There are also many general references to the civil wars, as when Clarence dreams that he and Richard had 'cited up a thousand heavy times,/During the wars of York and Lancaster,/That had befallen us' (I.4.14–16). There is not much reference to the earlier historical events which had led to the civil wars, but in one place Rivers, about to be executed at Pomfret, remarks that it was here that Richard II had been murdered (III.3.8–12), thus reminding us of the original act of usurpation by the Lancastrians which had led to the later conflicts. This constant recalling of the past makes us feel that the characters are trapped in a web of historical events: until the crimes of the past have been expiated, and the guilty punished, there will be no peace in England, and even the innocent will suffer.

Besides constantly recalling the past, the play looks forward to the future, by means of prophecies, curses, dreams, and omens. Richard refers (IV.2.94–7) to a prophecy by Henry VI that Richmond would one day be king, an episode depicted by Shakespeare in *3 Henry VI*. Richard also recalls (IV.2.102–6) a prophecy by 'a bard of Ireland' that he would not live long after seeing Richmond (which he had interpreted as a place-name). Much commoner than prophecies, however, are curses; and the arch-curser is Margaret: she curses Clarence (I.3.136), Edward IV (I.3.196), Prince Edward (I.3.198–200), Queen Elizabeth (I.3.201–8), Rivers and Dorset (I.3.209–13), Hastings (I.3.210–13), and Richard (I.3.215–33). All these curses, except the one on Dorset, are fulfilled in the course of the play, and the characters in question usually remember the curse and recognise that 'poor Margaret was a prophetess' (I.3.300). She does not curse Buckingham, but warns him against Richard; he disregards the warning, and suffers the fate she had predicted, as he himself recognises (V.1.25–7). Margaret herself had been cursed by the Duke of York when she helped to murder Rutland; Richard reminds her of this, and points out that these curses have been fulfilled (I.3.173–80).

Characters also in effect curse themselves, when they make solemn protestations which they have no intention of honouring. Buckingham, for example, swears his loyalty to Queen Elizabeth and her kindred, and begs God to punish him through the treachery of one of his own friends if ever he breaks his oath. He does break it, in helping Richard to depose Elizabeth's son; later, when he is being led to execution, he remembers his 'feigned prayer', and acknowledges that God has given him in earnest what he had begged 'in jest' (V.1.12–24).

Omens are referred to by Hastings when disaster overtakes him: his horse had stumbled three times that day on the way to the Tower (III.4.84–6). More significant are dreams—those of Clarence, Stanley, Richmond, and Richard. Most of Clarence's dream (I.4.9–63) is an expression of his agonised fear and remorse at his past sins; but the early part of the dream, in which Richard knocks him overboard, is prophetic, though Clarence does not understand it, and thinks that Richard's action is an accident. Stanley dreams that the boar (Richard) tears off his helmet (III.2.11), and takes this as a warning; Hastings ridicules his fears (III.2.26–7, 72–3), but later sees that they were justified (III.4.82–3). The dreams of Richard and Richmond (V.3.119–77), in which the ghosts of Richard's victims appear to them, are prophetic, pointing to the outcome of the following day's battle.

Like the evocation of the past, the successful prediction of the future makes us feel the inevitability of events, the inexorable process of history. But it also suggests that supernatural forces are at work, and that events are governed by God's providence.

Dramatic irony

Ordinary irony consists in saying the opposite of what is meant; but by dramatic irony we usually mean the effect obtained when words or events mean more to the audience than to a character on the stage. There is dramatic irony when Hastings tells Stanley's messenger that his 'good friend' Catesby will keep them informed about any danger; the audience knows that Catesby is an agent of Richard (III.2.22–4). Often there is a character on the stage who shares the audience's greater knowledge, and the irony may be deliberately produced and relished by that character. Because of Richard's hypocrisy and scheming, he has ample opportunity for dramatic irony. In I.1, he assures Clarence that he will 'deliver' him (I.1.115); Clarence takes this at its face value, but the audience knows what Richard really means. When Prince Richard of York asks Richard for his dagger, he replies 'My dagger, little cousin? With all my heart' (III.1.111); for the audience, who know Richard's plans, this has a sinister meaning which is not understood by the young princes. Hastings, because of his blindness, is a great source of dramatic irony, which is relished by Catesby:

HASTINGS: Well, Catesby, ere a fortnight make me older,
          I'll send some packing that yet think not on't.
CATESBY: 'Tis a vile thing to die, my gracious lord,
          When men are unprepared and look not for it.
                                      (III.2.60–3)

The audience knows, but Hastings does not, that it is Hastings himself that Catesby is referring to. Later in the scene, Buckingham joins in the game, when he jokingly tells Hastings that he has no need of a priest, because he has 'no shriving work in hand' (III.2.112–14).

The dramatic irony is sometimes emphasised by asides, which underline for the audience the fact that some characters on stage have knowledge which is hidden from others. Richard is particularly fond of asides, as when he comments on Prince Edward's kingly ambitions— 'Short summers lightly have a forward spring' (III.1.94); in this case the remark is made even more pointed by rhyme. Richard's supporters, once again, also join in, as with Buckingham's 'And supper too' (III.2.121), and Catesby's 'For they account his head upon the Bridge' (III.2.70), which is made the more telling by Hastings's innocent reply— 'I know they do, and I have well deserved it' (III.2.71). The dramatic irony and the asides increase the sense of deceit and hypocrisy in the play, the gap between appearance and reality; but they are used, especially by Richard, with great relish, and they contribute to our sense of his wit and intelligence.

The figures of rhetoric

Poets in Shakespeare's time were greatly influenced by classical rhetoric, and especially by the figures of speech. Figures were defined as departures from normal usage for artistic effect, and covered an enormous range of different things, from the smallest stylistic detail (such as the use of a non-normal variant of a single word) to the mode within which a whole work operated (such as imprecation). There were two main types of figure, *tropes* and *schemes*. Tropes were figures in which there was some kind of substitution or transfer of meaning, the basic type being metaphor; they included irony and allegory. Schemes were figures in which there was no such substitution or transfer or meaning. In grammatical schemes the normal linguistic rules were broken (for example by non-normal word-order, or breaking off a sentence and leaving it unfinished). In rhetorical schemes there was no such breaking of the rules of grammar or syntax. Rhetorical schemes included a wide range of different things, including verbal patterns and elaborate set pieces (such as descriptions of people or places).

Late sixteenth-century poets loved the figures, and so did their readers. Handbooks were written defining and illustrating them, and the number of different figures described could run to as many as a hundred and fifty. Poets made lavish use of figures of all kinds, but in the 1580s and 1590s they were particularly fond of the rhetorical schemes which consisted of verbal patterns, produced by repetition. Shakespeare is no exception: in his early works, like *Richard III*, he makes great use of figures, often very elaborate ones, and is particularly fond of verbal patterns. Such patterns are found in the speeches of many of the characters, and are often unobtrusive: for example, in the long speech made by King Edward after the announcement of Clarence's death, there is a series of questions beginning with the word *Who* (II.1.108–10), followed by a series of questions beginning with the words *Who told me* (II.1.111–16); but these repetitions do not call attention to themselves, and seem like a quite natural expression of the King's grief and anguish. In some passages, however, the patterns are extremely elaborate and obvious. This is especially so in lamentations, like the following:

Q. ELIZABETH:	Ah for my husband, for my dear lord Edward.
CHILDREN:	Ah for our father, for our dear lord Clarence.
D. OF YORK:	Alas for both, both mine, Edward and Clarence.
Q. ELIZABETH:	What stay had I but Edward? And he's gone.
CHILDREN:	What stay had we but Clarence? And he's gone.
D. OF YORK:	What stays had I but they? And they are gone.
Q. ELIZABETH:	Was never widow had so dear a loss.
CHILDREN:	Were never orphans had so dear a loss.
D. OF YORK:	Was never mother had so dear a loss.
	Alas! I am the mother of these griefs.
	Their woes are parcelled, mine is general.
	She for an Edward weeps, and so do I;
	I for a Clarence weep, so doth not she;
	These babes for Clarence weep, and so do I;
	I for an Edward weep, so do not they.

(II.2.71–85)

Especially when used, as here, with different speakers, these elaborate patterns produce a choric effect. Because a number of people contribute to the pattern of words, what is said seems independent of any individual speaker. This introduces an impersonal note into the play: something is being said which is not said by any individual, and which therefore appears to be said by something or somebody outside or above the characters. The patterns help to evoke an order, a moral order, and suggest the hierarchical society which is one of the expressions of this order.

Indeed, one of the reasons for the popularity of this kind of elaborate verbal pattern in the later sixteenth century may well have been that it reflected the ordered hierarchical world to which people were clinging, as it became increasingly threatened. The time when figures of this kind become less popular, around 1600, is precisely the time when people are becoming conscious of the growing moral, social, and political crisis which was to lead to the breakdown of the old order.

Besides being found in laments, elaborate verbal patterns occur in Margaret's curses and denunciations (see I.3.187–232). One of the effects, again, is to make her curses seem more than simply personal: the patterns contribute to the feeling that she is the voice of nemesis, an inevitable doom. What she says (a reminder of the wrongs and violence of the past) is obviously important; but the ritualistic way in which it is said makes it seem more than merely human.

Richard himself often uses relatively simple and unrhetorical language: this is seen in his conversation with the murderers (I.3.340–54), where his speech is notably unpatterned. When he does use elaborate and obvious patterns, they are usually a part of his acting: he uses them, for example, when he is playing the part of the devoted lover to Anne (I.2.179–82). He also uses verbal repetition for satirical purposes, as when he puns on 'noble' and 'marry' (I.3.80–1, 97–9), and this produces quite a different effect, attacking order rather than evoking it. It is true that patterns sometimes occur in his soliloquies, as when he repeats the word *I* in his opening speech (I.1.14–24); but it is to be noted that this is patterning of the unobtrusive kind, and seems to the audience a quite natural reflection of Richard's egotism. In one place, moreover, Richard deliberately destroys a piece of elaborately patterned rhetoric spoken by Margaret: she is cursing him, and concludes with a series of lines beginning with the word *Thou*, ending thus:

> MARGARET: Thou loathed issue of thy father's loins,
>   Thou rag of honour, thou detested—
> RICHARD: Margaret.
> MARGARET: Richard.
> RICHARD: Ha?
> MARGARET: I call thee not.

>   (I.3.231–3)

There Richard interrupts Margaret's curse, inserting her name into it instead of his own; and when she tries to complete it with his name, he pretends to believe that she is simply addressing him.

As might be expected, then, Richard, the individualist who attacks the established order, does not use the highly elaborate verbal patterns found in the speech of some of the characters, except when he is acting. But there is an interesting case in the dream scene before Bosworth. The dream itself is highly formal and patterned, the different ghosts using similar phrases, and ending with similar curses on Richard and encouragements to Richmond (V.3.119–77); this is the kind of pattern associated with the moral order. But when Richard starts out of his dream in terror, he uses a very different kind of language:

> Give me another horse, bind up my wounds:
> Have mercy Jesu. Soft, I did but dream.
> O coward conscience! how dost thou afflict me?
> The lights burn blue. It is now dead midnight.
> Cold fearful drops stand on my trembling flesh.
> What? do I fear myself? There's none else by.
> · (V.3.178–83)

That indeed uses rhetorical devices, but it is not formal or patterned. On the contrary, it is fragmented, broken into short phrases, and sounds like the tortured utterance of an individual—a single will and a single conscience. So the mode of speech in the scene corresponds to what the speakers stand for: the ghosts, with their patterned speech, represent hierarchy and the traditional moral order; Richard, with his broken incoherent phrases suggestive of real speech, is an individual character in conflict with that order. But later in the same speech Richard's language becomes highly patterned:

> My conscience hath a thousand several tongues,
> And every tongue brings in a several tale,
> And every tale condemns me for a villain;
> Perjury, perjury, in the highest degree,
> Murder, stern murder, in the direst degree,
> All several sins, all used in each degree,
> Throng to the bar, crying all 'Guilty, Guilty'.
> (V.3.194–200)

Here it is Richard's conscience speaking, and his conscience is an expression of the moral order; it is fitting therefore that at this point he should use the obtrusively patterned language associated with that order: his conscience is the voice of that order accusing him.

The poetry of the play

Richard III is almost entirely in verse. There is just one passage in prose, when the two murderers of Clarence talk to one another (I.4.99–163), but when Clarence wakes up they switch to verse. Prose is used here as being suitable for such plebeian characters, especially in a passage of rather low emotional tension. In some plays, Shakespeare uses a good deal of prose, with various functions, but not in *Richard III*: on their previous appearance, the murderers use verse (I.3.341–54), and verse is also used by the three citizens (II.3) and the scrivener (III.6).

The verse used in the play is nearly all blank verse, that is, unrhymed iambic pentameter. An iambic pentameter has the following basic pattern:

> ᴗ / ᴗ / ᴗ / ᴗ / ᴗ /
> To strut / before / a wan-/ton amb-/ling nymph
> (I.1.17)

The line consists of five metrical units (called *feet*) each consisting of an unstressed syllable followed by a stressed one. On this basic pattern the poet makes variations, and may depart quite a long way from it. Two common variations are the inversion of a foot, and the use of a foot consisting of two unstressed syllables. Both are seen in the opening line of the play:

> / ᴗ ᴗ / ᴗ ᴗ ᴗ / ᴗ /
> Now is / the win-/ter of / our dis-/content
> (I.1.1)

There the first foot is inverted, and the third foot consists of two unstressed syllables. In his later plays, Shakespeare often uses very free rhythms in his blank verse, but in early plays like *Richard III* the variations are never so great as to obscure the underlying pattern.

Occasionally, rhyme is used, especially at the end of a scene, giving a sense of finality. The same use of rhyme to suggest finality is seen at the end of the last speech of the Duchess of York (IV.4.195–6), when she tells Richard that he will never see her again. Richard himself sometimes uses rhyme for humorous effect, making his comments more pointed and witty (I.2.262–3; III.1.79, 93–4, 185).

Shakespeare makes great use in the play of the figures of rhetoric (see above), especially rhetorical schemes of words (verbal patterns). The use of patterns makes the style expansive rather than rapid, dwelling on a subject rather than hurrying onward. This leisurely cumulative kind of style is seen in such set pieces as Clarence's account of his dream (I.4.1–63) and Edward IV's lament for the death of Clarence (II.1.104–34). There is, nevertheless, a good deal of variety of style in the play, and Richard in particular often uses a much plainer, more colloquial, and more rapid style (I.3.323–54; II.1.136–41, III.1.151–200).

In most of Shakespeare's plays there are recurrent groups of words (often referred to by critics as *images*) that affect the atmosphere of the play and point to the themes that it is handling. In *Richard III*, Richard is frequently compared to an animal, especially a dog, but also a spider, toad, boar, and hog; these images suggest a repulsive brutality; the toad and the spider, moreover, are linked with poison, to which he is also compared. There are also references to Hell, devils, and demons, and Richard in particular is compared to a devil. There are many references to trees, orchards, gardens, herbs, weeds; in particular, the royal family is compared to a tree, and the members of the family to its leaves, flowers, or fruit. There are also many references to storms and tempests, usually as images of violent disorder and conflict in human society. And throughout the play there are references to the Tower of London; many scenes take place in the Tower, or just outside it, and we are constantly reminded of the infamous deeds which have taken place in it, so that the Tower becomes a threatening symbol for dark and bloody deeds.

Part 4

Hints for study

General advice

You must know the play really well: read it time and time again. You should know it so well that, if you are asked a question about it, you can immediately think of events or characters that help you to answer it, and quote short passages from memory. When you write about the play, show that you know it well: support your argument by detailed reference to what happens in the play, and with short quotations. Read the play at different speeds: at first, you will sometimes want to work through it slowly, using the notes, to make sure that you understand everything; but remember that it is a play, so sometimes read it straight through without a break; and try to imagine it being acted as you read it, or even act it out yourself, reading aloud.

Secondly, you should *think* about the play. There are different views on what it means, how effective it is, how Shakespeare gains his effects, and so on. In the end, you yourself must decide what you think about these things. Obviously you want to know what other people have said about the play, and in Part 5 below there are some suggestions for further reading; but the final test for any view is to be found in the text of the play itself. So when you are thinking about the play, have the text open in front of you, and constantly check whether the view you are considering is borne out by what is said and done in the play. Do not make up your mind too quickly, or accept immediately the view of some critic; first weigh all the evidence you can find in the play. It is especially necessary not to shut your eyes to evidence that contradicts your own current view; on the contrary, you should look for such evidence, and see where it leads you. Indeed, unless you develop the habit of considering the evidence that contradicts your own view, you will not be *thinking* at all.

Thirdly, you must practise writing about the play. You need to be able to write simply and clearly, to arrange your material methodically, and to present evidence for your viewpoint. Sometimes you should write an essay at leisure, with the text of the play open in front of you. But if you are working for an examination you should also practise writing essays under examination conditions—in a limited time, and without the text of the play. Here are some suggestions for topics to study, followed by some essay questions.

Topics for study

(1) Does Richard's character change in the course of the play? In particular, compare Act I with Act IV from this point of view.

(2) Go through the play collecting examples of Richard's play-acting, noting what role he is enacting on each occasion. Is there any change in the course of the play?

(3) Analyse the character of (a) Clarence, (b) King Edward IV, (c) Hastings, (d) Buckingham, (e) Stanley (Derby), (f) Richmond. In each case, examine what the character says, what he does, and what other people say about him.

(4) Analyse the characters of Prince Edward and Prince Richard of York. Do they talk and behave like children?

(5) Consider the functions in the play of the various female characters.

(6) Examine the following scenes or episodes, and say what (if anything) they contribute to the total effect of the play: (a) Act II Scene 3; (b) Act III Scene 3; (c) Act III Scene 6; (d) Tyrrel's description of the murder of the princes (IV.3.1–22).

(7) Go through the play looking for references to events which took place before the play began. What effect do they have?

(8) Go through the play looking for examples of (a) Richard's humour, and (b) his vivid use of language.

(9) Examine the references in the play to *dogs*. What are they used for? Look similarly at the references to (a) other animals, (b) Hell, devils, and demons, (c) trees, and (d) storms.

(10) Look through the play to see how often *priests* appear on the stage, or are referred to. What effect does their presence have?

(11) Examine all references in the play to *dreams*. What is their importance?

(12) Examine all the references in the play to *conscience*. Which characters are troubled by their consciences, and with what outcome?

(13) Analyse the following speeches: (a) Richard's opening soliloquy (I.1.1–41); (b) Margaret's curses on the court (I.3.187–232); (c) Clarence's account of his dream (I.4.9–63); (d) Edward IV's speech about the death of Clarence (II.1.104–35); (e) Tyrrel's account of the murder of the two princes (IV.3.1–22); and (f) Richard's soliloquy after awakening from his dream (V.3.178–207). With each speech, examine the course of its argument, any changes of mood or tone or attitude that take place in it, the kinds of effect it produces, and the methods used to produce them (look at metaphors, comparisons, rhetorical devices).

(14) Collect all the evidence you can find in the play suggesting that we are meant to have at any rate some sympathy for Richard. Does this sympathy cast doubt on the role of the play as an expression of conventional Tudor views on the events depicted?

Essay questions

If you have worked at the play in the ways suggested above, you should be able to tackle the following essay questions. They are arranged roughly in order of difficulty, and more elementary students are advised not to tackle the later ones.

(1) In *Richard III*, how is it that we can be interested in Richard, and even sympathetic towards him, when he is so completely wicked?

(2) What do we learn about Richard (a) from his wooing of Anne, (b) from the way he deals with Hastings, and (c) from his behaviour when he awakes from his dream on the night before Bosworth (including his conversation with Ratcliffe)?

(3) Discuss the role of Queen Margaret in the play, including in your answer a comparison of her character (a) with that of Richard, and (b) with that of Queen Elizabeth.

(4) Do you agree that, in *Richard III*, the central character changes after he has become king? Support your view by detailed reference to the play.

(5) Discuss the theme of conscience in *Richard III*, and its relation to other themes in the play.

(6) Give an account of the methods which Shakespeare uses to reveal Richard's character to us, and to shape our attitudes towards him.

(7) Discuss the role of dreams in *Richard III*, and their contribution to the overall effect of the play.

(8) 'The elaborate patterns worked out in it [*Richard III*] give it an exceptionally firm sense of structural unity' (Nicholas Brooke). Give an account of these 'elaborate patterns', and consider their functions.

(9) *Richard III* makes much use of patterned speech. Does this have a function in the play? Does the play contain any other types of speech?

(10) 'The theme of *Richard III* is the wounds of civil war and their cure.' How adequate do you find this as a description of the play?

(11) Examine the view that *Richard III* is a tragedy rather than a chronicle or history play.

(12) '*Richard III* appears on the surface to underwrite the Tudor Myth, but in fact in many subtle ways it undermines it.' Discuss this view, including a brief introductory paragraph on 'the Tudor Myth'.

Writing an essay

When you write an essay, write about the subject set, and about nothing else. If you are asked a question on the character of Richard, do not discuss the life of Shakespeare, or sixteenth-century politics, or the Elizabethan stage: if you do, your examiner will just cross such passages out, and you will have wasted time and effort. Do not even take it for granted that your essay has to have some kind of introductory paragraph. Students are often taught that an essay must begin with an introduction and end with a conclusion; but this is not necessarily so, and the introductions that students write are often mere padding. If you are asked to write an essay on the subject 'Does the character of Richard change in the course of the play?', the best way to begin your essay is with some such words as 'At the beginning of the play Richard is . . .'; this gets you straight into the subject without fuss or waste of time. But before you begin, read the question carefully, and make sure that you understand it; notice, for example, that question (6) above does not ask you to describe Richard's character; it asks you about the *methods* which Shakespeare uses to present this character, and that is quite a different question (including, for example, such things as recurrent images, and the use of soliloquy and asides).

Moreover, your essay must be planned. Do not start writing without thinking, but first jot down ideas; then arrange these under headings, which will provide the sections of your essay; and note down suitable examples or quotations under each heading. When you have the plan of the essay clear, begin writing. Try to write in a plain, straightforward way, but nevertheless with enthusiasm: an essay usually reads better if we feel that the writer is enjoying what he is talking about.

Specimen essay plan

As an example of a simple plan for an essay, let us take the first essay subject from our list: 'In *Richard III*, how is it that we can be interested in Richard, and even sympathetic towards him, when he is so completely wicked?'. After jotting down ideas, you might arrive at a plan such as the following: (1) Single-mindedness; (2) Energy; (3) Wit; (4) Language; (5) Acting; (6) Zest; (7) Limitations of sympathy.

Under these seven headings can be grouped the various ideas and examples that have been thought of, and you will get a fuller plan. Given the plan, the essay can be made of various lengths, according to the amount of detail and illustrative material which is included. The following version is about a thousand words long. Notice how use can be made of very short quotations; this is especially useful in examinations.

Specimen essay

Wicked people can quite well possess qualities which we normally admire, and this is the case with Richard III. One such quality is Richard's commitment, his single-mindedness: he knows what he wants, and is unwavering in his pursuit of it. He has made his moral choice, as he tells us in the first scene of the play ('I am determined to be a villain'), and he is fully committed to it. Even at the end of the play, when he is facing disaster—threatened by supernatural forces, and tormented by his conscience—he refuses to repent or change his mind; he stands by his choice to the very end, leading his men 'If not to heaven, then hand in hand to hell'.

With this commitment goes an enormous energy. He is always busy, always planning, always bustling. He acts with speed and decisiveness: when he decides, after his coronation, to marry off Clarence's daughter and to dispose of his own wife, these plans are immediately carried out, as we hear in the very next scene; when Buckingham hesitates to agree to the murder of the princes in the Tower, Richard at once writes off Buckingham and arranges the murder by himself. Richard's energy, moreover, is also an intellectual energy: we feel that his intelligence is greater than that of his opponents, that his triumphs over them are triumphs of the mind. In his soliloquies, when he is planning his future moves, we have the sense of a mind buzzing with energy and excitement: this is so, for example, in the soliloquies in the opening scene, where he plans Clarence's death, and again in the soliloquy which follows the wooing of Anne.

Richard also gains admiration because he is a highly entertaining character, and this makes him especially popular in stage performances. Two of the things which make him entertaining are his wit and his use of language, which are closely linked. The wit tends to be sardonic, as when he decides to send Clarence to Heaven (that is, to kill him), and adds as an afterthought 'If heaven will take the present at our hands'. The humour often arises from the ignorance of the person he is addressing, who understands only part of Richard's meaning: when Clarence is on the way to the Tower, Richard says to him 'I will deliver you, or else lie for you'; the audience knows in what way Richard intends to *deliver* ('free') his brother, but Clarence takes it at its surface meaning. Richard is also fond of puns, as when he puns on *naught* ('nothing' and 'wickedness') to Brackenbury, and on *noble* ('nobleman' and 'coin worth a third of a pound') when he is attacking the Queen's upstart relatives. The wit is often made more pointed by rhyme, as when he mocks Hastings in his suggestion that he should 'Give Mistress Shore one gentle kiss the more'.

Even when he is not joking or punning, Richard's language is often vivid and vigorous. In a play where the writing is on the whole formal and patterned, Richard introduces a vigorous and colloquial note, using trenchant and concrete metaphors. Speaking of the way he had worked for Edward IV, he says: 'I was a packhorse in his great affairs'. The relatives of the Queen who (he alleges) have slandered him to the King are called 'silken, sly, insinuating Jacks', with the implication that they are over-dressed and of lower-class origins. Commenting on Clarence's imprisonment, he says that he is 'franked up for fatting' (like a hog awaiting slaughter). He praises the murderers because their eyes drop millstones, whereas fools' eyes drop tears. This last example was proverbial, and Richard's language, with its concreteness, trenchancy, and alliteration, often reminds us of proverbs and popular sayings.

Above all, however, the spell that Richard casts over the audience is due to his love of acting, and his superb skill as an actor. He is constantly playing a role, putting on an act. To Clarence, he plays the part of the devoted brother; to Anne, that of the devoted lover. At court, he has many roles—the innocent man wrongly accused, the plain blunt man who cannot flatter, the other-worldly simpleton. He even acts to his closest ally and confidant, Buckingham, pretending that Buckingham is the brains of their enterprise and its leader. The high point of Richard's histrionic career is perhaps the marvellous scene where he appears on the roof between two bishops, playing the part of the devout and other-worldly man without ambition, while Buckingham tries to persuade him to accept the crown, and Richard pretends to refuse. The wholehearted-ness with which he throws himself into the parts he acts is seen in one delightful phrase in this passage, when he mildly rebukes Buckingham for using an oath: 'O do not swear, my lord of Buckingham'.

And with this point we have come full circle: we are back to the single-mindedness and commitment with which we started; for Richard throws himself completely into his acting, as into everything else he does. But he not only throws himself into what he does: he also enjoys it. There is an enormous zest about him. He enjoys his own cleverness, his own jokes, his own successes, his own acting. This enjoyment often comes out in his soliloquies, for example the one that follows the wooing of Anne, where he triumphs at this incredible victory, 'All the world to nothing', and comments sardonically that he must after all be a very handsome fellow, 'a marvellous proper man'. But the zest comes out in almost everything he says and does, and is one of the reasons for his attractiveness as a stage character.

But despite our enjoyment of Richard's performances, and our admiration for his remarkable qualities, we are always aware that he is an evil character—a complete egotist, a cold-blooded murderer, a man who has rejected love and indeed all human ties. Occasionally, perhaps, as we enjoy his humour or his acting, we take a holiday from ordinary morality, and even identify ourselves with his Machiavellianism and destructiveness. In the end, however, we have to condemn him, and recognise that all his brilliant gifts are used for wicked purposes, that he is indeed a 'cacodemon', a 'bottled spider', a 'poisonous bunch-backed toad'. But nothing is just black and white, and in the play there is a certain tension, a hint of ambiguity: the most wicked character in the play is also the most brilliant and attractive; and perhaps, therefore, *Richard III* can be regarded as a tragedy.

Part 5

Suggestions for further reading

The text

Line references of *Richard III* used in these Notes are taken from:

HONIGMANN, E. A. J. (ED.): *Richard III*, (The New Penguin Shakespeare) Penguin Books, Harmondsworth, 1968.

There are two larger annotated editions which have full notes and substantial introductions:

DOVER WILSON, J. (ED.): *Richard III*, (The New Cambridge Shakespeare) Cambridge University Press, Cambridge, 1971.

HAMMOND, A. (ED.): *Richard III*, (The Arden Shakespeare) Methuen, London, 1981.

Collected works of Shakespeare

The standard one-volume modern-spelling edition of Shakespeare is the following:

WELLS, STANLEY and TAYLOR, GARY (EDS): *The Complete Works*, Clarendon Press, Oxford, 1986.

There are innumerable simpler and less expensive editions. The following is a convenient one-volume edition with a reliable text:

ALEXANDER, P. (ED.): *The Complete Works*, Collins, London and Glasgow, 1951; paperback edition, HarperCollins, Glasgow, 1994.

Critical works

CLEMEN, W.: *A Commentary on Shakespeare's Richard III*, Methuen, London, 1968. This gives a detailed scene-by-scene analysis.

More advanced students will find sections or chapters on *Richard III* in many other works on Shakespeare, especially in books on the history plays. The following are recommended:

BROOKE, N.: *Shakespeare's Early Tragedies*, Methuen, London, 1968.

CAMPBELL, L. B.: *Shakespeare's 'Histories': Mirrors of Elizabethan Policy*, Huntington Library, San Marino, California, 1947.

KNIGHTS, L. C.: *Shakespeare: The Histories*, Longman, London, 1962.

PALMER, J.: *Political Characters of Shakespeare*, Macmillan, London, 1945.

REESE, M. M.: *The Cease of Majesty*, Edward Arnold, London, 1961.

TILLYARD, E. M. W.: *Shakespeare's History Plays*, Chatto and Windus, London, 1944.

TRAVERSI, D.: *An Approach to Shakespeare: Vol I, Henry VI to Twelfth Night*, third edition, Hollis and Carter, London, Sydney and Toronto, 1968.

WAITH, E. M. (ED.): *Shakespeare: The Histories*, Prentice-Hall, Englewood Cliffs, New Jersey, 1965.

On Shakespeare's imagery, consult the following:

CLEMEN, W.: *The Development of Shakespeare's Imagery*, second edition, Methuen, London, 1977.

SPURGEON, C.: *Shakespeare's Imagery*, Cambridge University Press, Cambridge, 1935; reprinted Beacon Press, Boston, Mass., 1958.

On Seneca, and his influence on Shakespeare, see:

CUNLIFFE, J. W.: *The Influence of Seneca on Elizabethan Tragedy*, London, 1893.

LUCAS, F. L.: *Seneca and Elizabethan Tragedy*, Haskell House, New York, 1969.

On the rise-fall pattern in Shakespeare's tragedies, consult Lecture II in:

BRADLEY, A. C.: *Shakespearean Tragedy*, Macmillan, London, 1904; third edition by J. R. Brown, Macmillan, Basingstoke, 1992.

Sources

For the sources of the play, consult the relevant portions of the following:

BULLOUGH, G.: *Narrative and Dramatic Sources of Shakespeare*, Vol III, Routledge and Kegan Paul, London, 1960.

MUIR, K.: *The Sources of Shakespeare's Plays*, Methuen, London, 1977.

Dictionaries

The standard authority on the meanings of English words in the past is the great twenty-volume *Oxford English Dictionary* (second edition, 1989). More convenient for the elementary student of Shakespeare is the following:

ONIONS, C. T.: *A Shakespeare Glossary*, enlarged and revised throughout by Robert D. Eagleson, Clarendon Press, Oxford, 1986.

Background works

An elementary account of the official world-view of Shakespeare's time will be found in:

TILLYARD, E. M. W.: *The Elizabethan World Picture*, Chatto and Windus, London, 1943.

For an account of the English language in Shakespeare's time, and the ways in which it differed from present-day English, see:

BARBER, C.: *Early Modern English*, Deutsch, London, 1976.

On the theatres, companies, actors and stage conditions of Shakespeare's time, consult:

GURR, A.: *The Shakespearean Stage 1574–1642*, Cambridge University Press, Cambridge, 1970. This gives a very useful, though tightly-packed, account.

A useful general reference book is:

BAYLEY, PETER: *An A·B·C of Shakespeare*, (Longman York Handbooks) Longman, Harlow, 1985. New edition, 1993.

The author of these notes

CHARLES BARBER was educated at St Catharine's College, Cambridge, where he won the Charles Oldham Shakespeare Prize. After a year's teacher-training at the University of London, where he won the Storey-Miller Prize for Educational Theory, he became a teacher at a London grammar school. During the war he served in the Royal Air Force. He was then lecturer in English at the University of Gothenburg, Sweden, assistant lecturer in English at the Queen's University of Belfast, and from 1959 until his retirement in 1980 he was at the University of Leeds, where he eventually became a Reader in English Language and Literature, and Chairman of the School of English. His publications include an edition of Shakespeare's *Hamlet*, editions of three plays by Thomas Middleton, and a number of books on the English language, including a popular Pan paperback called *The Story of Language*.

York Notes: list of titles

Choice of Poets
Nineteenth Century Short Stories
Poetry of the First World War
Six Women Poets

CHINUA ACHEBE
Things Fall Apart

EDWARD ALBEE
Who's Afraid of Virginia Woolf?

MAYA ANGELOU
I Know Why the Caged Bird Sings

MARGARET ATWOOD
Cat's Eye
The Handmaid's Tale

JANE AUSTEN
Emma
Mansfield Park
Northanger Abbey
Persuasion
Pride and Prejudice
Sense and Sensibility

SAMUEL BECKETT
Waiting for Godot

ALAN BENNETT
Talking Heads

WILLIAM BLAKE
Songs of Innocence, Songs of Experience

ROBERT BOLT
A Man For All Seasons

HAROLD BRIGHOUSE
Hobson's Choice

CHARLOTTE BRONTË
Jane Eyre

EMILY BRONTË
Wuthering Heights

ROBERT BURNS
Selected Poems

GEOFFREY CHAUCER
The Franklin's Tale
The Merchant's Tale
The Miller's Tale
The Nun's Priest's Tale
Prologue to the Canterbury Tales
The Wife of Bath's Tale

SAMUEL TAYLOR COLERIDGE
Selected Poems

JOSEPH CONRAD
Heart of Darkness

DANIEL DEFOE
Moll Flanders
Robinson Crusoe

SHELAGH DELANEY
A Taste of Honey

CHARLES DICKENS
Bleak House
David Copperfield
Great Expectations
Hard Times
Oliver Twist

EMILY DICKINSON
Selected Poems

JOHN DONNE
Selected Poems

GEORGE ELIOT
Middlemarch
The Mill on the Floss
Silas Marner

T. S. ELIOT
Selected Poems
The Waste Land

HENRY FIELDING
Joseph Andrews

F. SCOTT FITZGERALD
The Great Gatsby

E. M. FORSTER
Howards End
A Passage to India

JOHN FOWLES
The French Lieutenant's Woman

BRIAN FRIEL
Translations

ELIZABETH GASKELL
North and South

WILLIAM GOLDING
Lord of the Flies

OLIVER GOLDSMITH
She Stoops to Conquer

GRAHAM GREENE
Brighton Rock

WILLIS HALL
The Long, The Short and The Tall

THOMAS HARDY
Far from the Madding Crowd

Jude the Obscure
The Mayor of Casterbridge
Selected Poems
Tess of the D'Urbervilles
L. P. HARTLEY
The Go-Between
NATHANIEL HAWTHORNE
The Scarlet Letter
SEAMUS HEANEY
Selected Poems
ERNEST HEMINGWAY
The Old Man and the Sea
SUSAN HILL
I'm the King of the Castle
BARRY HINES
A Kestrel for a Knave
HOMER
The Iliad
The Odyssey
ALDOUS HUXLEY
Brave New World
BEN JONSON
The Alchemist
Volpone
JAMES JOYCE
Dubliners
A Portrait of the Artist as a Young Man
JOHN KEATS
Selected Poems
PHILIP LARKIN
Selected Poems
D. H. LAWRENCE
The Rainbow
Sons and Lovers
Women in Love
LOUISE LAWRENCE
Children of the Dust
HARPER LEE
To Kill a Mockingbird
LAURIE LEE
Cider with Rosie
CHRISTOPHER MARLOWE
Doctor Faustus
ARTHUR MILLER
The Crucible
Death of a Salesman
A View from the Bridge
JOHN MILTON
Paradise Lost I & II
Paradise Lost IV & IX
TONI MORRISON
Beloved
ROBERT O'BRIEN
Z for Zachariah

SEAN O'CASEY
Juno and the Paycock
GEORGE ORWELL
Animal Farm
Nineteen Eighty-four
JOHN OSBORNE
Look Back in Anger
WILFRED OWEN
Selected Poems
HAROLD PINTER
The Caretaker
SYLVIA PLATH
Selected Works
ALEXANDER POPE
Selected Poems
J. B. PRIESTLEY
An Inspector Calls
JEAN RHYS
The Wide Sargasso Sea
WILLY RUSSELL
Educating Rita
Our Day Out
J. D. SALINGER
The Catcher in the Rye
WILLIAM SHAKESPEARE
Antony and Cleopatra
As You Like It
Coriolanus
Hamlet
Henry IV Part I
Henry V
Julius Caesar
King Lear
Macbeth
Measure for Measure
The Merchant of Venice
A Midsummer Night's Dream
Much Ado About Nothing
Othello
Richard II
Richard III
Romeo and Juliet
Sonnets
The Taming of the Shrew
The Tempest
Twelfth Night
The Winter's Tale
GEORGE BERNARD SHAW
Arms and the Man
Pygmalion
Saint Joan
MARY SHELLEY
Frankenstein
RICHARD BRINSLEY SHERIDAN
The Rivals
R. C. SHERRIFF
Journey's End

RUCKSHANA SMITH
Salt on the Snow

MURIEL SPARK
The Prime of Miss Jean Brodie

JOHN STEINBECK
The Grapes of Wrath
Of Mice and Men
The Pearl

ROBERT LOUIS STEVENSON
Dr Jekyll and Mr Hyde

TOM STOPPARD
Rosencrantz and Guildenstern are Dead

JONATHAN SWIFT
Gulliver's Travels

ROBERT SWINDLES
Daz 4 Zoe

MILDRED D. TAYLOR
Roll of Thunder, Hear My Cry

W. M. THACKERAY
Vanity Fair

MARK TWAIN
Huckleberry Finn

VIRGIL
The Aeneid

ALICE WALKER
The Color Purple

JAMES WATSON
Talking in Whispers

JOHN WEBSTER
The Duchess of Malfi

OSCAR WILDE
The Importance of Being Earnest

TENNESSEE WILLIAMS
Cat on a Hot Tin Roof
A Streetcar Named Desire

VIRGINIA WOOLF
Mrs Dalloway
To the Lighthouse

WILLIAM WORDSWORTH
Selected Poems

W. B. YEATS
Selected Poems